Amazon Advertising:

An Author's Guide to Selling More Books - How to Make Your Ads Work

Copyright © 2019 Stan Lock

Contents

Introduction

Let's get straight to the point. If you are (or want to become) an independent publisher, you have entered the world of business. Whether you like it or not, you will have to become involved with marketing your product in one way or another, either by doing it yourself or by paying somebody else to do it for you. You might just get lucky and find that you simply publish your book on Amazon and it just takes off. Possible? Yes. Likely? No. In 2019 and beyond, it's getting ever closer to impossible. The need to market your book has become pretty much a requirement if you want to make any sales. Amazon Advertising (formerly known as AMS) gives us the opportunity to market our books directly to the customers that are actually buying.

Amazon Ads have made life somewhat easier for marketers with no experience. Take note, "somewhat easier" doesn't necessarily mean easy. Unfortunately, it's becoming increasingly more difficult to sell anything on Amazon without using Sponsored Ads and I'm not just talking about books. The bottom line is this; if you want to sell your book on Amazon then you really need to start understanding Amazon advertising, and in order to do this, we really need to take a few steps back and think more about selling in general and how marketplaces like Amazon work. If you are looking for a book that shows simple steps that walk you through setting up a sponsored ad and producing guaranteed results, then this is not the book for you, it's not possible. There is no simple or guaranteed method: every book, every genre, just about everything you do with your advertising can be different for every author and every book, if for no other reason than we all think and do things differently. If you want "simple," then just setup a sponsored ad with auto targeting and hope for the best. At this moment in time, this does sometimes work, but I expect it will become increasingly more difficult in the not-so-distant future. The more you learn to optimise for relevancy, the more chance you have of your ads working for you. We'll get to all of this throughout the rest of this book.

This book is not a step by step course. It is not designed to take you from being a complete beginner to becoming an expert. A lot of what I talk about in here is the result of a certain amount of analysing and reverse engineering Amazon search and Advertising. I don't claim to know everything, but more importantly you should understand that the Amazon system changes regularly. What is accurate today could quite possibly change tomorrow. Changes are often subtle but you should always be aware of them. Either way, if you are a compete beginner looking for an easy guide to using and setting up Amazon ads, this is probably not the book for you.

Images

There are a lot of images and screenshots used throughout this book. As mentioned above, the system and layout changes regularly. Just within the time I have been writing this book, quite a few things have changed already. Where possible I have included and updated screenshots to reflect these changes but there may still be a few that are using slightly older images where I cannot recreate the same data. With that in mind, some of the layouts might look a little different to what you are seeing on your own screen, especially if you use a small computer monitor or tablet. Unless a certain functionality has changed or been removed completely I'll still use some older screenshots so if you can't see something ... just look for it.

For instance, on the old advertising dashboard many of the tabs and buttons have been moved from the top of the screen to the side. This might sound harsh but if you cannot figure this kind of stuff out yourself then you are already in trouble. If you want your ads to perform well then you need to have at least a slightly curious and analytical mind and if you can't figure out something then ask questions. There are plenty of groups on Facebook and social media where others are glad to help. Consider it a requirement of running long term successful advertising.

One more word about images. If you are reading this on a Kindle device or App then the images may look too small or hard to read. Double clicking / tapping on them should enlarge them. You might also need to switch between portrait and landscape if the images are too small. If you are reading this on a cell phone then you are very unlikely to make the images clear and easy to read. Good luck if you can but you're probably wasting your time. Just be realistic, 4 inch screens are not designed for stuff like this.

Amazon Search

This is a food for thought section, but very important to grasp.

If you want to make your advertising work for you then you will need to spend some time thinking about things from the buyer's perspective. Imagine for a moment that you walk into a large, multi-storey superstore, each floor the size of a football pitch. The only thing this superstore sells is books. The first floor is well lit and has aisles and departments for many book categories. Obviously you would have an idea of the kind of book you are looking for so you head for that department and follow the signs that lead you closer towards your preferred genre until you reach a few large shelves with hundreds of books for you to choose from. Let's say you are looking for romance novels. You find them, look through them, but nothing really catches your eye. You then see a sign that says "more romance novels upstairs," so you decide to go up there to take a look.

When you get up there you realise that this floor isn't as well laid out as the ground floor and it's also not so well lit, you have to work a little bit harder to find something. You don't spend too much time here because it's not inspiring you but you see yet another sign, "more romance novels on the second floor". Maybe you will give up at this point or maybe you are determined and decide to go up to have a look. The second floor is much like the first, only now there are no shelves, just tables. Each table has a huge pile of books, much like a jumble sale, it's a complete mess. At best, you might have a quick skim over what's laying on top of the pile but you don't waste much of your time. You decide to go back downstairs, you see another sign on the way that says "more romance novels on the third floor". You decide not to bother, you don't even go there. The top floor gets very few, if any, visitors and all of the books up there never even get seen. This is the real world analogy of Amazon. Something about staring at a computer screen when you are shopping on-line makes it harder to realise this reality.

We can demonstrate this with a few examples. Forget about books for the moment, let's have a look at a popular product sold on Amazon so that we can start to understand how difficult it can be to get your product merely seen by shoppers.

Let's say you want to buy a USB flash drive. If you were to go to your local superstore you might find they have a large range to choose from, maybe twenty, fifty or even something crazy like a hundred. Now go to Amazon.com and type "USB flash drive" into the search. Here's what I see at the top of the page: "1-16 of over 10,000 results for "usb flash drive". Think about that for a moment? That's ten thousand results. The search results only show 20 pages with 16 products on each page. This means Amazon is deciding I can only view 320 of the 10,000 possible results.

Maybe I have something wrong or Amazon is finding 10k results that aren't actually flash drives. Perhaps some of those 10,000 items are other products that mention the words "usb flash drive" as part of their description. So let's test it and see what happens. I'll start by using the filters and click on 32GB where it says "Flash drive capacity".

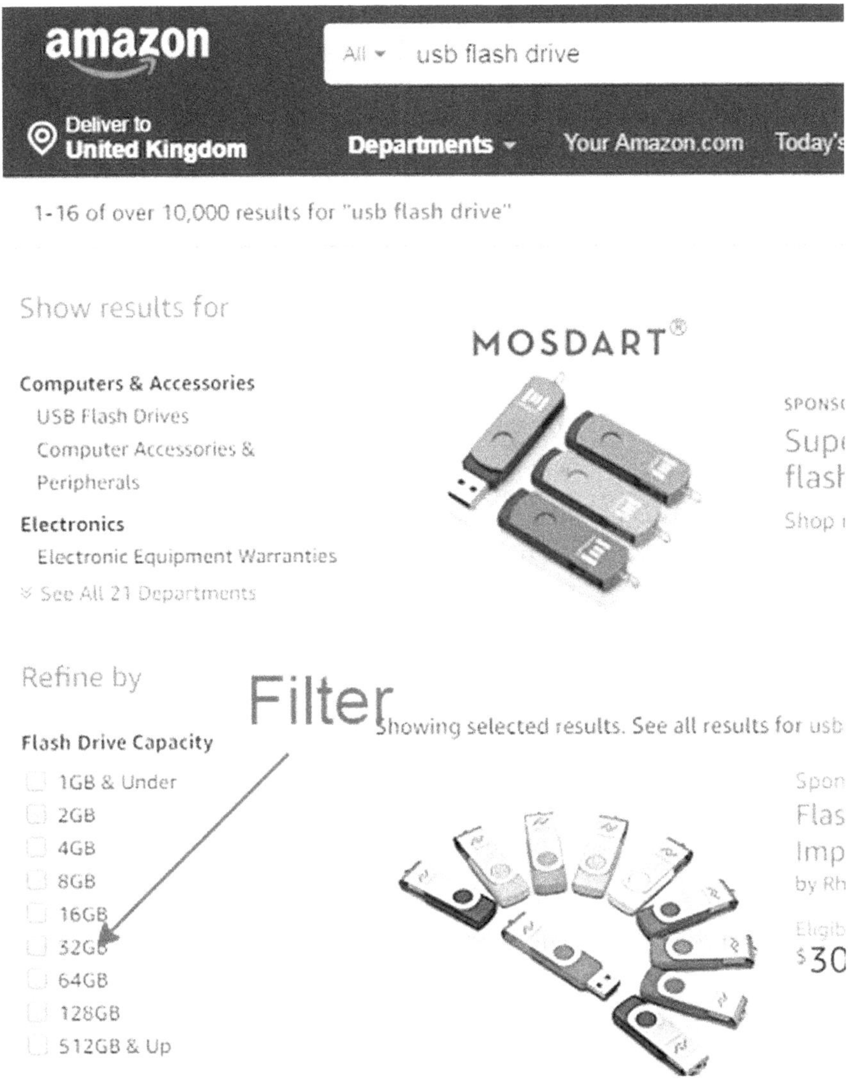

Show results for

MOSDART®

Computers & Accessories
  USB Flash Drives
  Computer Accessories &
  Peripherals

SPONSC
Supe
flasf

Electronics
  Electronic Equipment Warranties

Shop

⌄ See All 21 Departments

Refine by

Filter

Showing selected results. See all results for usb

Flash Drive Capacity

☐ 1GB & Under
☐ 2GB
☐ 4GB
☐ 8GB
☐ 16GB
☐ 32GB
☐ 64GB
☐ 128GB
☐ 512GB & Up

Spon
Flas
Imp
by Rh

Eligib
$30

I now get 9,000 results with 380 pages. Sure enough, as I click through each page I am seeing flash drive after flash drive. Let's jump right along to page 100 and see what's there. It's crazy, banana shaped flash drives, spanner shaped, flash drives on a pendant, for key-rings and the list goes on. Let's jump to page 300 and have a look. Same again, flash drive after flash drive, literally thousands.

Note: If you want to quickly jump to another page in the search results, first go to page 2. Then in the address bar look for where it says "&page=2" and change the 2 to whatever page you want and hit Enter. You might get a string of text much longer than the shown in the image below with more than one occurrence of "page=", if so just go right to the end and scroll back until you find the first occurrence.

Getting back ... I did choose a product that I knew would be very popular in the hope of making you see just how important this is. What would you do if you wanted to buy a flash drive from Amazon? You might be more specific and perhaps type something like "32gb usb keyring flash drive". Let's try it ... "115 results". OK that's not so bad. Some people would just type 32g or 32 instead of 32GB. Let's try a few searches and see what comes up.

32g usb keyring flash drive = 16 results
32 usb keyring flash drive = 120 results
32gb flash drive = over 2000 results
32 flash drives = over 3000 results
Flash drive 32gb = over 2000 results
usb flash drive pendant = 187 results
usb flash drive red = over 1000 results

Now bear with me, it's vital that you understand all of this even though we're not yet talking about books. Whether you are selling electronic gadgets or books, the principles remain the same. With Amazon, your book is not a small fish in a big pond, it is a spec of sand in the Sahara Desert as far as getting seen is concerned (well, maybe not quite that big but you get the point). You must never assume that just because something is listed on Amazon, somebody will see it. It may never get seen by anybody, not ever.

To get sales, we need to narrow things down with the objective of getting seen by potential buyers, this is obviously the very first thing we need to achieve. If we were selling a 32GB USB flash drive we would have very little chance of getting seen among 2000 results if "32GB USB flash drive" were the only keyword phrase we were relying on. We are on the 14th floor of the superstore analogy. To make sales on a product this competitive we'd need to get smart and experiment. To be honest, something this popular would likely need a lot of money thrown at it if you were selling a generic flash drive with no specific or unique features. Even then, the features would need to be something buyers are actually searching for. Most people aren't this specific, whether that be gadgets or books. They type in fairly generic search phrases and often buy what gets thrown up on page one, or more likely another product shown in the product detail page. Why? Because Amazon lists the most popular selling items for that key phrase. Let's assume most people don't care much about the look or shape of a flash drive and 80% (hypothetical but very possible percentage) of all buyers end up purchasing either 32gb or 64gb. Amazon will show the most popular selling items in these two sizes right there on page one of the search. That's 80% of your potential buyers already done and gone. It takes a long time, experience and lot of money to sell anything with a massively popular keyword like this so we don't go there. Maybe some other day, but not now. We want to go after the remaining 20%, or more likely an even smaller percentage of that 20%, so we drill down.

When you type search terms into the Amazon search bar (from the home page) you should see other suggestions in the drop-down. Something like this:

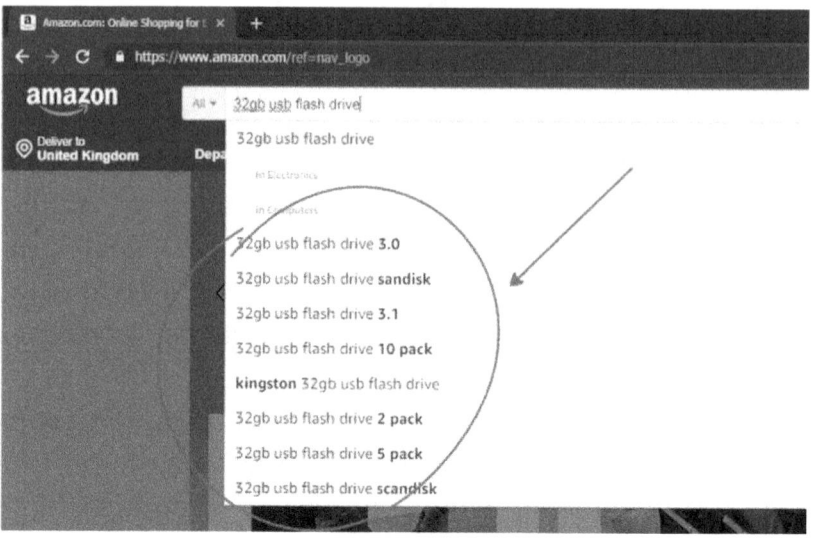

You can experiment with these by drilling down with various search phrases. These are valuable because they are terms that people actually use. With some playing around I found "usb flash drive for girls". This gives 251 results which is much more hopeful for us to have a chance of getting seen. If you can make that fit your product then you might be in with a chance. First we need to make Amazon's algorithms think this is a suitable match. We would do this by including "girls" in the title, the description and 7 keyword fields (see chapter "Categorisation"). Also add any other features, if any, that might be typically related with girls, such as "pink" (as long as that's actually the colour of it) or "lipstick" if it's in a lipstick shaped container, etc. Amazon's algorithms are smart enough to know these other kinds of keywords are commonly associated with girls.

Getting these details in place doesn't just affect your organic search alone, they also have an effect on your Ad's relevancy and increase the chance of your Ad showing up and getting impressions. You cannot make your Ad show up by bid price alone. If Amazon does not think your product suitably matches your keywords then you can be the highest bidder and still get very few impressions. This is a very important thing to realise, you have to get many factors right for your Ad to perform well. I'll give you an (extreme) example. If I type "usb flash drives" then I get "over 7000 results in 12 departments" or in other words, Amazon is showing 12 categories in which usb flash drive might belong to, as shown in the below image.

Now let's do the same search from the Kindle Store. (Select the different departments from the drop-down in the search bar)

We see two technical books about flash drives. Now let's do the same search again in "Books"

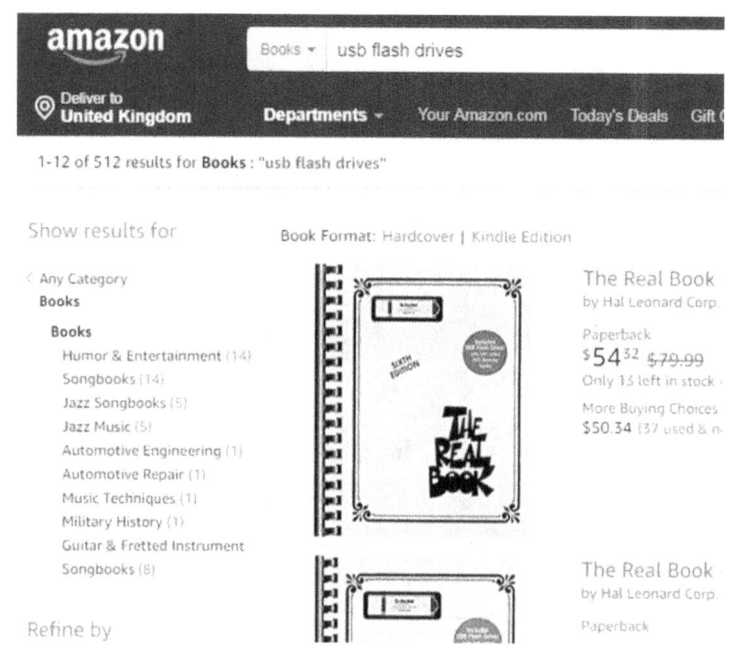

Now we get 512 results in various book categories, most of which are books that include audio on a flash drive.

Let's do one more. From the home page (all departments) we'll use the search term "usb flash drives book"

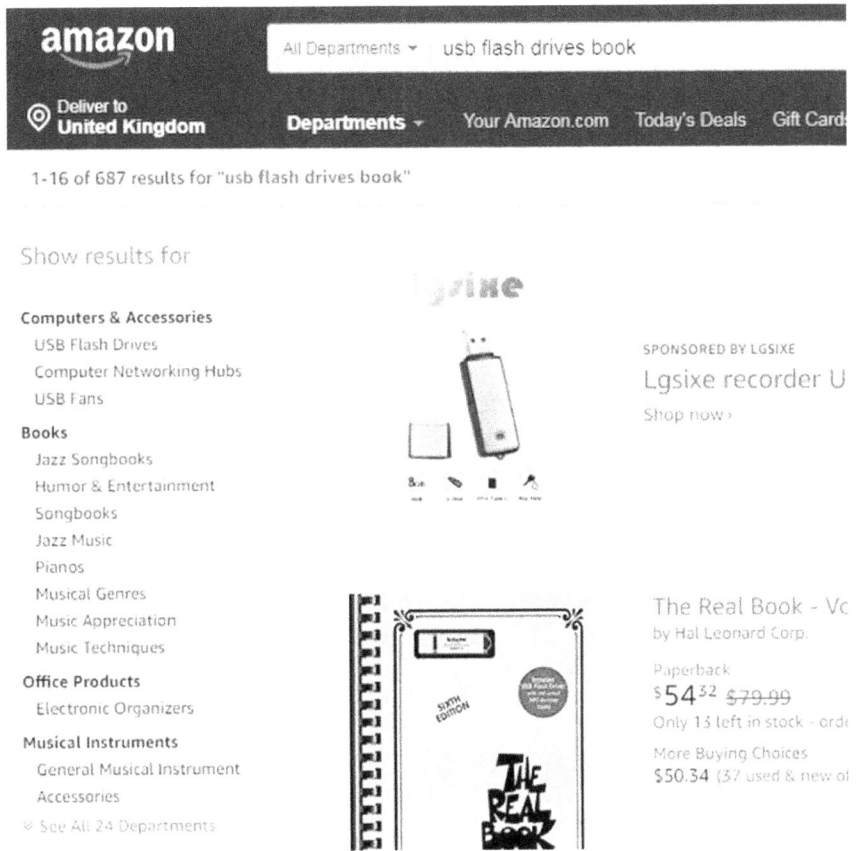

Now we get 687 results in various categories, not just books. Why is this important? Because Amazon algorithms make assumptions. It tries to figure out what you are "probably" looking for, not what you might actually be looking for. I did say this was an extreme example but just like the "spec of sand in the Sahara" analogy, you need to think about things like this in order to fix things when you are not making any sales or getting many impressions with your Sponsored Ads.

If you do not have much experience with selling and advertising in markets such as Amazon then it's very easy to overlook these fundamentals. Let's see if we can demonstrate this with something a little less obvious. From the home page (All Departments), do a search for "AMS for authors" . . . we get this:

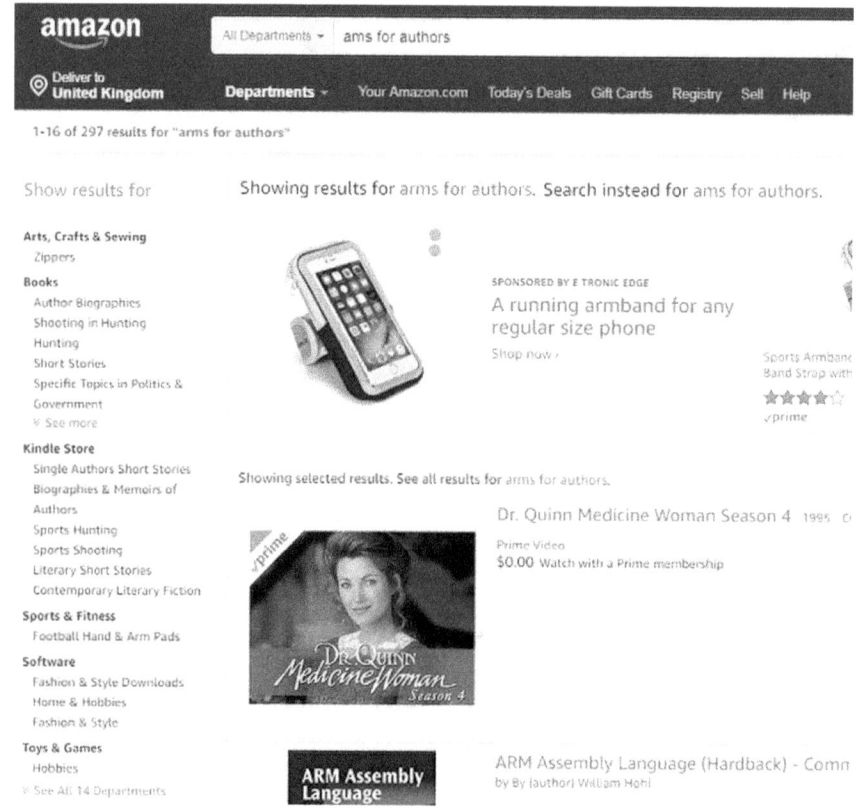

Not what you'd expect? Look at the results where it says "showing results for *arms* for authors" If I were to be selling a book about AMS ads for authors then I'd expect that to be a fairly good keyword phrase. Well, not according to Amazon. To be honest I think Amazon doesn't yet have enough information gathered for this keyword because AMS Ads is (surprisingly) not a very popular book topic. I suspect it will be over the next year or two, but not yet in early 2019 (note to self, why am I writing this book?). OK, let's click where it says "search instead for ams for authors"

I won't bother showing an image here but here's what I get; 101 results, the first three books shown are about AMS ads and the rest is an assortment of completely non-related books and two more books reasonably related. Page two of the results are showing books on subjects ranging from electric shock therapy to model engineering and nowhere to be seen is Brian Meeks or Mark Dawson's book on AMS Ads, probably the two most popular in the topic at present. AMS for authors is clearly a very bad keyword and yet you'd expect it would be the opposite. Let's continue.

We'll now try "Advertising for authors," again from the home page. OK, the first three results are pretty much what you'd expect. Brian Meeks is at the top and the next two are about AMS Ads and Marketing books on Amazon. But that is it. The rest of the page is showing me a cup, a book about dentistry and mp3 audio for piano background music. Seriously? Pages two and three of the search results are a mixture of books about writing, advertising, more cups (go figure?) and best of all, a poster of Clint Eastwood.

If we now do the same search from the books category, the results are looking a bit more sensible and if we do the same again from the Kindle Store, things are better still. Take note: Where your buyer is searching from, i.e., from the homepage or the books category or Kindle store etc., can drastically change the results, yet my guess is many people's searches start out right from the home page, therefore not all keywords are equal. As this relativity closes in, things start showing more as expected but again, always remember the extreme examples because when things get closer aligned, it becomes harder to spot the obvious.

Let's go again. This time we'll start from Kindle eBooks, You get here by going to "Departments," choose "Kindle Store" and then "Kindle eBooks" should appear below the search bar or in the left column. Do a search for "Advertising for authors". Page one shows us books that are now more like what we would expect, although still a few missing from the results that I'd expect to be there and some that, although seem slightly relevant, aren't as relevant as the books that will show up if you search instead for "AMS ads for authors".

There are a few more interesting things you will find in these search results. Brian Meeks' book "Mastering Amazon Ads" is quite clearly the most popular book at present on this topic. He has a new book called "Mastering Amazon Descriptions" which is still only for pre-order. At the time of writing, Brian's book is not set for release for another few days, yet this book is showing on page one for most of the searches above. Another interesting thing is the search term "AMS ads for authors" or simply "AMS ads" show one of his other books "Underwood, Scotch and Wry". If you have read Mastering Amazon Ads then you will have noticed Underwood, Scotch and Wry is mentioned quite a few times as one of his test examples. Are Amazon also using a books actual content to try creating relevancy? Quite possible. There is also the possibility that the Amazon algorithms are just connecting Brian Meeks' books with AMS ads as he seems to have the monopoly on this term at the moment. My guess is probably both.

So what can we learn from all of this and how can it help us sell more books and make our AMS adverting (and organic search) work for us? It's all about understanding relevancy and making sure Amazon's algorithms don't confuse what your book should be about. This is all discussed in the following few chapters.

Fiction and Non-Fiction

There is a world of difference between selling fiction and non-fiction books. To some extent, non-fiction books in many categories are about the easiest thing to sell on Amazon, as long as you aren't selling in a hyper-saturated market like Weight Loss, etc. Even then I'd argue it's possible if you put enough effort into it, although wouldn't recommend it without any advertising experience.

The good thing about non-fiction is most of the subjects are about how to do, or understand, something. This lends itself well to buyers searching many variations of keywords and phrases that are quite specific. We can tap into the less competitive keywords in the hope of getting seen. This may get us a few sales and start building momentum for the book.

Fiction is a bit different. Many readers will search for very broad terms that are virtually impossible to compete with if you aren't already a high ranking or known author. Longer, more specific keyword phrases will get searched for but they are difficult to find. For fiction, a keyword generator tool, something like KDP Rocket can be invaluable for finding keywords that might work for your book. You've probably already heard of it, or use it, but otherwise just search on-line for KDP Rocket by Dave Chesson.

For non-fiction books, something like KDP Rocket can still be very useful but I would be a little more careful with the keyword list and pick out the ones that seem most relevant. Too much irrelevancy can actually harm your results in Amazon organic search as well as Amazon ads. The same goes for fiction but it's harder to guess what keywords will work and what might not. Either way, pick out the obvious (non-relevant) ones and delete them. For example, if your book is a detective mystery for adults then be careful to avoid keywords that would suggest it's for teens. You also may find a keyword generator will pull phrases like "How to become a detective". Get rid of things like this (unless it's your actual book title, in which case it might be worth rethinking a different title if the book is fiction), it will harm your click through rate and if by chance you get a few sales, it will confuse Amazon's algorithms in deciding whether your book is fiction or non-fiction. The more relevant you are, the longer your AMS ads will work and the more consistent your book will come up in the search results for related searches.

Likewise, if you have a non-fiction book about learning to play the piano for beginners then make sure all your keywords are relative to piano for beginners and watch out for keywords like "advanced" or "intermediate" etc. If your book is aimed at learning for kids then make sure you don't include words like "adult". Although many of these are obvious, some are not always so. If you are unsure then just try the search for yourself in Amazon and see what results come up. Make sure you do the same search from the Amazon's home page as well as from "books" and "Kindle Store" departments. Also make sure you do this search while logged out and in private browsing or incognito mode from your web browser.

Categorisation

It's hard to know just how many books are for sale on Amazon. I've seen it suggested that it was over 32 million in June 2014. While I don't know how accurate this information is, it wouldn't surprise me if this is true. Let's see if we can find something more definite by trying to find a book with a very low sales rank (low as in sales, i.e., best seller rank with a high number). It seems to me the obvious way to search for something like this would be look for a book that's probably too out of date for anybody to want. I guess something like "Microsoft Office 95" would be a book fitting that description so let's search for that.

Result from page 1 in search:
Microsoft Office for Windows 95 Resource Kit
Amazon Best Sellers Rank: #12,407,411 in Books

Result from page 3 in search:
Microsoft Office for Windows 95: Short Course
Amazon Best Sellers Rank: #21,066,912 in Books

If sales rank is to be believed (which I have no reason why not) then these two books are at 12+ and 21+ million down in the list of books on Amazon. Therefore 30+ million books might just be believable. Let's say, however, that 32 million isn't a true picture because of things like new editions, hardback, paperback, spiral bound etc., will all have different ISBN numbers and so on. Let's agree that it's very plausible there are over 20 million books titles for sale on Amazon. That's a lot of books to get yours seen amongst. Obviously this is why we have categories. Most people, however, don't browse categories, they use the search box and they look at "also-boughts" and sponsored ads from other books they are currently viewing. Even if they did browse through categories, the popular ones could have something like 10k to 50k books listed in each. That is a lot of noise for you to cut through to get your book seen by anybody.

Competition aside, the way to help getting your book seen is by making sure the Amazon algorithms have it categorised optimally because even if a lot of people do not browse categories directly, it's a determining factor for where and when your book shows up to potential readers. When somebody is viewing the detail page of any book, they are, to some extent, effectively browsing the categories that book belongs to, via recommendations and the various carousels. A lot of variables can affect how relevant your book will be to the search algorithms. Many of these we don't know about, all we can do is guess, but the main ones are quite obvious, these are the things Amazon actually tell us about.

1. Book title
2. Book Subtitle
3. Book category
4. Keywords
5. Sales Rank.
6. Sales history

There will be other things like reviews and author rank but we can only deal with what we have direct control over. This will be the first four in the list above. For fiction, the book title and subtitle are not so easy to work with. If you can somehow incorporate keywords into them then maybe do so, not forgetting to check Amazon's terms about what you can and cannot include in the title (look at KDP help pages for "Metadata Guidlines" for ebooks as well as paperback). Most of the time it's probably not worth the effort with fiction books as it's far more important to make the title and subtitle sound appealing to potential readers. There's no point in improving your search visibility if it gets counteracted by a poor title that's uninspiring.

Non-fiction is far more suited to keywords in the title and subtitle. If you have a book about "How to Play the Piano" then there is nothing wrong with giving it that exact title, it not only describes the book but is also a strong keyword phrase. For the subtitle you could do a mix of keywords and try to make it a bit of a hook. Let's say your keyword research brings up terms like "piano chords," "scales for piano," "piano for beginners" etc., then the subtitle could go something like "Learn Piano Chords and Scales Ideal for Beginners". You could probably come up with something more appealing than that but that's the general idea. Just make sure that what you write accurately describes your book otherwise you will get poor reviews and a high refund rate, both of which will eventually hurt your search ranking.

The main thing to understand here is that when your book is newly published, it's mostly, if not all, categorised by computer algorithms. Imagine this was a library and the librarian is trying to figure out which shelf to put your book on. A human can look at the cover, quickly read the synopsis and make a fairly good guess at what the book is about and where it belongs. Computer algorithms aren't so smart. They try to figure this out from the keywords and categories that you supply. If you try to add too many keywords to appeal to a broader audience then you might be confusing the algorithms and make it difficult to narrow down. This is quite important because with millions of readers, Amazon tries to target the readers that it knows will be looking for your kind of book. The less defined or the more varied the information you give it, the less chance that Amazon will know exactly who to target.

A lot of authors assume this is not important because they see top selling books in irrelevant categories and showing up for all sorts of seemingly non-relevant search terms. Remember, you are not those authors, you don't have that luxury. These authors already have a following. When they launch a book it sells quite well just from their following. Amazon already knows the type of reader that this author appeals to and then figures out, through those sales, the type of reader that is buying. This gives the book some kind of assumed relevancy that probably outweighs other factors.

When you are a fairly unknown author with no following, you can't afford to be so non-specific with categorising and choosing keywords for your book. The closer you get to being relevant, the more chance there is of Amazon showing your book to the correct audience. If you are targeting the right readers then once you get a few sales then your relevancy increases and you will show up more to the right audience.

Category and Keyword Settings

You choose your book categories and keywords when you first publish your book. These can be changed any time you like. Categories can be entered or changed from your KDP dashboard by editing the book's details.

In here, scroll down and you will find two sections, one for keywords and one for categories.

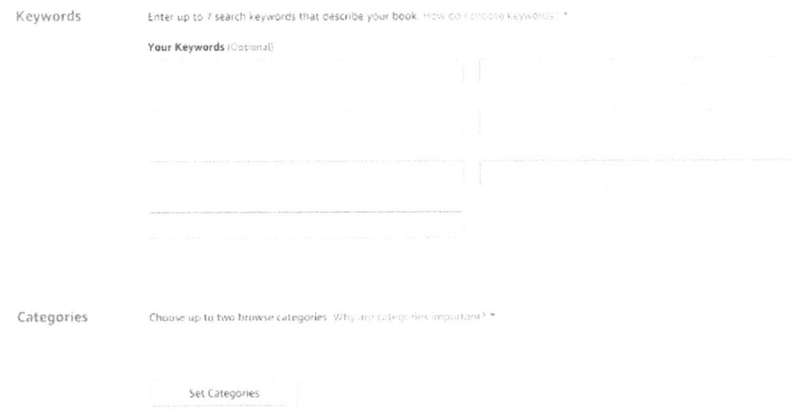

When you set your categories, you only get two to choose from. You'll need to decide for yourself which categories are best for your book. It's always a good idea to check the categories of other books similar to yours and try to get listed in similar categories. You can check the competition's categories from their book detail pages on Amazon, it will look something like this, about halfway down the page.

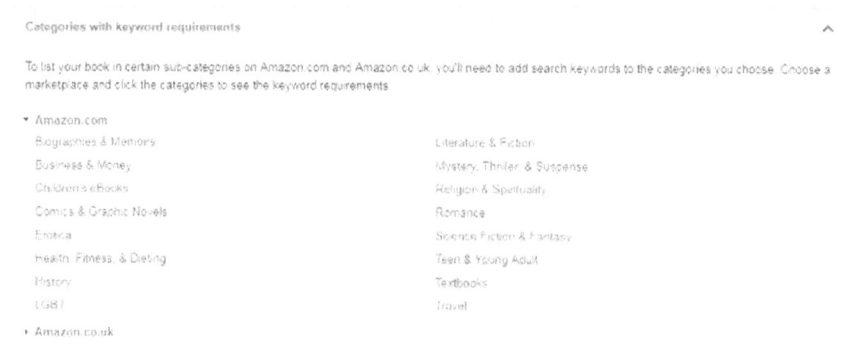

Shipping Weight: 1.2 pounds (View shipping rates and policies)
Average Customer Review: ★★★★☆ ∨ 744 customer reviews
Amazon Best Sellers Rank: #2,663 in Books (See Top 100 in Books)
    #71 in Books > Science Fiction & Fantasy > Science Fiction > **Hard Science Fiction**
    #108 in Books > Science Fiction & Fantasy > Science Fiction > **Alien Invasion**
    #120 in Books > Science Fiction & Fantasy > Science Fiction > **First Contact**

You may find that you cannot choose these same categories from the category list so you'll just have to get as close as you can. You may also be able to get into more specific categories by using certain keywords in the keyword fields. You will find these listed in the KDP help pages. Here's a link to it:

https://kdp.amazon.com/en_US/help/topic/G200652170

Amazon change pages often so if this does not work for you then look through the KDP help pages for "Selecting Browse Categories" and then down the page look for "Categories with keyword requirements".

Categories with keyword requirements

To list your book in certain sub-categories on Amazon.com and Amazon.co.uk, you'll need to add search keywords to the categories you choose. Choose a marketplace and click the categories to see the keyword requirements.

▾ Amazon.com

Biographies & Memoirs   Literature & Fiction
Business & Money   Mystery, Thriller & Suspense
Children's eBooks   Religion & Spirituality
Comics & Graphic Novels   Romance
Erotica   Science Fiction & Fantasy
Health, Fitness, & Dieting   Teen & Young Adult
History   Textbooks
LGBT   Travel

▸ Amazon.co.uk

Click on one of the categories, let's say we want "Mystery, Thriller and Suspense," this will bring up a keyword list that looks something like this:

Category	Keywords
Mystery, Thriller & Suspense Characters/Amateur Sleuth	amateur
Mystery, Thriller & Suspense Characters/British Detectives	british detective
Mystery, Thriller & Suspense Characters/FBI Agents	fbi
Mystery, Thriller & Suspense Characters/Female Protagonists	female protagonist
Mystery, Thriller & Suspense Characters/Police Officers	police
Mystery, Thriller & Suspense Characters/Private Investigators	private investigator
Mystery, Thriller & Suspense/Crime Fiction/Heist	heist, robbery, thief, theft
Mystery, Thriller & Suspense/Crime Fiction/Murder	murder
Mystery, Thriller & Suspense/Crime Fiction/Noir	noir
Mystery, Thriller & Suspense/Crime Fiction/Organized Crime	mob, mafia, organized crime, yakuza

Find the category you want on the left and then copy the keywords from the right and paste it into one of your keyword fields. Let's say we want the category for .../Crime Fiction/Heist. Look at the keywords next to that category and paste them right into one of the keyword fields like so:

Keywords	Enter up to 7 search keywords that describe your book. How do I choose keywords? *
	Your Keywords (Optional)
	heist, robbery, thief, theft

You can use more keyword fields to try capture more categories and you can also populate them with search terms you would like to show up for, or a mixture of both. As always, don't forget to check the guidelines for words that should be avoided. Things like other author names are no longer allowed in your keywords fields. All of this can be found in the KDP help pages.

There are seven of these keyword fields available. Throughout this book I will refer to them as keyword metadata or 7 keyword fields.

You should think carefully about the categories and keywords you hope to show up for. If your book is in a very competitive genre then you should spend some time trying to find suitable categories (if possible) that are less competitive. The same attention should be paid to your use of keywords. This can be easier said than done but if all else fails then make sure that you use appropriate and relevant category and keywords, no matter what. This is more important than anything. If you start veering away from relevancy then you will likely have a harder time getting your book shown to the right people.

Populating these keywords fields gives Amazon's algorithms a good sense of what your book is about. You can use up to 50 characters per keyword field. A lot of people recommend you fill this section up with as many keywords as you can. I'd take that recommendation with caution. Far better to keep as relevant as possible. If you can only find a few keywords that are relevant, then just use those few. If you can think of hundreds, then as long as they are truly relevant then use them all. My personal opinion is that fewer, very relevant terms will work better in the long term. One idea is to just use a few keywords here and then monitor your advertising search term reports over time. Once you have a good collection of keywords that lead to sales, these will often be a good fit for entering in the keyword fields. There's no rush here, you can add or change these keywords as often as you like. Don't however do too may big changes at one time. Change things slowly and gradual otherwise you might find a sudden turn in what's already working.

Relevancy and Algorithms

There is a lot of talk and differing opinions among authors when the topic of relevancy comes up. Some don't believe in it, some swear by it and others think it's all a big conspiracy and Amazon is out to take all of our money.

Relevancy is important, plain and simple. Remember there are over 20 million books on Amazon. If we type something into the search bar, browse a category or view the detail page of a particular type of book, then the Amazon algorithms need to be able to figure out what books to show you. It can only show you a tiny proportion of the 20m+ books. If I search for "murder mystery books" I don't expect to see any books about gardening or weight loss. This is obvious to all of us. Somehow or another, Amazon needs to understand what your book is about so that it can show it to the right audience.

None of us really know exactly how this is done. What we do know is it's probably not decided by humans, it's decided by computer algorithms. We can, however, make some assumptions that are likely to be quite probable. Computer algorithms are not magic and do not have the ability to think for themselves, at least not beyond what is programmed into them in the first place. Let's simplify things for a moment.

We've all, at some point, recommended books or movies to friends or had them recommended to us. We've done this either because we know the friend well enough that we have a good sense or what they like, or we've had discussions about particular topics that might prompt us to say something like "Oh, you should try reading ...". Amazon is no different. If you have purchased and browsed enough books on Amazon then they have collected information about you that it considers to be your interests. If I visit Amazon regularly and spend a lot of time browsing and sometimes purchasing books about self-help, then it knows that I'm interested in this subject. This is not too dissimilar to you knowing your friend's interests and recommending them a book. If I type something into the search bar, this is also not unlike having a conversation with a friend that prompts us to recommend them a book. If I type in "how to start a small business" it's like I'm saying to Amazon, "Hey, I'm interested in starting my own business, can you recommend any good books to me?"

Shoppers actions are effectively scored and stored. Amazon has collected, over the years, many millions of search terms, browsing and buying behaviours and it can make some pretty good guesses at what most people are looking for when they use certain search terms or browsing patterns. This part is quite easy, it just requires a lot of historical and trend data. The next part is also quite easy, it just needs to show all the books that are relevant to the search queries and browse patterns.

Depending on where the buyer is on the Amazon website, i.e., which department, category, search results or detail page, the books that get shown will range from the most popular sellers to new releases and an almost random scattering of other books that may or may not be related. I say "almost" random because I don't believe anything is random, it just appears to be. There is always a reason these outliers appear, most of the time we can figure out why with a little bit of digging. Sometimes it's simply the result of people (shady authors) trying to game the system. More often than not, however, it's the result of Amazon misinterpreting what the book is about and this, in turn, is the result of the author categorising incorrectly or using wrong, or not well-thought-out keywords. The bottom line here is if Amazon has your book categorised and understood properly then you will get shown to right audience at some point.

There is a world of difference between murder mystery novels and books on gardening. This is obvious. What's not always obvious, unless you really know your market well, is how much difference there is when the gap narrows between genres. For instance, how many people are there that read psychological thrillers but not sci-fi thrillers. It's important to know because it's very easy to confuse Amazon's algorithms to which category or precise genre that you belong. I have no idea what the typical behaviour of a fiction reader is but let's assume that those that read psychological thrillers rarely have any interest in sci-fi thrillers. If for some reason Amazon thinks your book is sci-fi (when it isn't) then it's going to try to show your book to those that are interested in this genre and you will struggle to make many sales. So how does it confuse your book?

At the end of the day it's nothing more than a computer program that tries to determine what your book is about. It figures this out by looking for words that are typically common to a particular genre, along with whatever information you supply yourself. Most of this is determined by the book title, subtitle, description plus the categories and 7 keywords fields used in the book settings in the KDP dashboard. I also suspect that to some extent, the text within the book is also used. Outside of the book itself is also customer behaviour and actions, which is probably the biggest determiner for relevancy. However, it's quite obvious that until you are actually getting sales, or views, then it's only the book details and keywords that are giving Amazon any sense of where and who to show your book to. This is why keywords and categories are very important to get right. You can test these by searching for books that you consider to be similar to yours and check what categories they belong to and what search terms they show up for. Try to get yours to match them. If the keywords you choose do not show similar books in search results then rethink whether you are using the best keyword choices.

Relevancy for Non-Fiction

The one thing that probably defines a book's relevancy more than anything else with Amazon is what people actually buy and download after using a particular search term and/or what they ultimately buy after browsing and clicking through various book categories and product detail pages. For instance, let's say the book is titled "How to Play the Piano". To us humans it is immediately obvious what this book is about. To Amazon algorithms it's probably very easy to figure out what this book is about and where to show it to potential readers, if we assume the following:

- The title is a strong keyword phrase.
- The subtitle uses words like "learn," "lessons" etc.
- The book description has keywords and phrases about learning piano.
- The 7 keyword fields (keyword metadata) were populated with terms like "learn piano".
- The two category choices were selected for the closest match.

It is almost certain that Amazon's algorithms relate words and phrases like "how to," "study," "learn," "learning," etc., so when it sees these kinds or words, it knows that the subject is about learning how to do something. It then sees the word "piano" and can assume this belongs to the musical instrument category. Amazon can now go about displaying your book among other books and search results that have similar attributes.

If people then click on your book and ultimately make a purchase, the algorithms can assume it must be shown in the right places and score, or mark it somehow as appropriate. If it continues to sell, then it probably gets scored higher for that category and similar keywords.

The above all seems fairly obvious and I doubt it's given you any light-bulb moments but we need to always keep these things in mind. It's very unlikely that you would write a book about how to play the piano and just call it "Piano" with no subtitle and only five words in the description that says "Learn all about the piano" while at the same time not bothering to fill in the keyword fields or choose relevant categories when setting up your book. If you did, Amazon might have a very hard time trying to figure out where best to show your book. Is the book about piano learning or piano tuning? It could be about servicing a piano or how to make a piano chair. The problem with things that are obvious, we tend to notice the two extremes but pay little attention to what's going on between because they aren't always staring us in the face. The in-between stuff can be very important, yet often overlooked.

The first example above is obvious because, well, it just is. "How to play piano" is clear to us and we assume it would also be clear to a computer algorithm. The second example, just "piano" is also clear to us that it is too vague, therefore it would come as no surprise to us if a search algorithm didn't quite know how to categorise it or where to display it. If you always keep these obvious extremes in mind, it makes it easier to spot potential problems with our book's optimisation within Amazon.

For example: If I decide to write a book about DIY guitar making. One idea I could use for a book title is "how to make your own guitar". Let's search that from Amazon's home page and see what we get:

1: How to make your own fingerpicking arrangements
2: How to make guitar amplifiers
3: DIY lap steel kit
4: **Build your own electric guitar**
5: Make your own basketball nets

6: Make leather guitar straps
7: **Make your own Spanish guitar**
8: How to memorize your fretboard
9: DIY Ukulele kit (Sponsored Ad)
10: How to teach guitar (Sponsored Ad)
11: Grand Theft Auto Sweatshirt
12: How to make music in your bedroom
13: Soprano Ukulele Kit
14: Barbie Sweatshirt
15: DIY Ukulele Kit
16: T Shirt (with picture of dog playing guitar)
17: AC adaptor for practice guitar amplifier
18: DIY Ukulele Kit
19: How to setup your guitar (Sponsored Ad)
20: How to play guitar with a capo(Sponsored Ad)
21: How to play guitar for adults (Sponsored Ad)

The list above shows the book titles listed on the first page of search results (I haven't named each book exactly as titled but close enough). The ones in bold are the only two books about making your own guitar. If I try the same search from the "books" department and the Kindle store, I get pretty much the same results so there is no point in listing them all here. The only oddity is when searching in "books" we get a few more sweatshirts in the results. I'm not even going to waste time trying to figure that one out!

There are two things to consider here. Either guitar making is very unpopular or "How to make your own guitar" is a bad choice of keyword that either gets few searches, or Amazon hasn't figured out what it means. If the keyword is bad for the search results then it will also (probably) be a bad choice for the title because we need to make the most of the words we choose in order to have more chance of showing up in the search. The book's title carries a lot of weight as far as keywords are concerned.

I'll now try a few more keyword ideas. To keep the following simple I'll do a few searches just from the "Books" department and score them from 1 to 16 in terms of relevancy; i.e., 3/16 would mean three books about guitar making and the rest non-related on a page of 16 results. I'll also ignore sponsored ads. I should also mention that all of these results (including the ones above) are done in private browsing, not logged in and using a VPN. This way Amazon can't use what it knows about me to influence the results.

How to make your own guitar: 2/9 (of 9 results)
How to build your own guitar: 12/14 (of 14 results)
How to build guitars: 11/16 (of 52 results)
Build your own guitar: 13/16 (of 39 results)
Guitar making: 15/16 (of 286 results)
Guitar building: 16/16 (of 232 results)
Building guitars: 15/16 (of 225 results)
Making guitars: 15/16 (of 277 results)
Guitar maker: 6/16 (of 234 results)
Luthier: 16/16 (of 449 results)

Carefully look through those results and you can see how some subtle differences can change the results quite drastically. The clear thing here is the big difference between the words "build" and "building" or "make" and "making". Not only does it produce more relevant search results, it also shows more total results. Our first choice only finds nine results in total with only two of them being relevant.

If you have no interest in music, you may be unsure what a luthier is? In short, a luthier is somebody who makes and repairs stringed instruments such as violins, guitars etc. It's a word we would likely use if we were selling a book about guitar making but would possibly be careful and not use it in the book title because this search term brings up a lot of results about building violins, as well as technical and engineering books which are very relevant to the profession, but not necessarily to the person that just wants to have a go at building their own guitar.

We could dig down and try to find many other keyword possibilities to add to the list above. I'm not going to do so here but if you were selling your own book then you would dig down further and find as many keywords as you can. Score them as above, or at least get a feel for them and make a list of all of the good words that get relevant results in the search with a decent amount of total results.

So how important is all of the above? There's a few things to think about. Relevancy is extremely important, without it your book will not get shown to the right people and ultimately not get many sales. The above, however, is not the only way Amazon gathers relevancy about your book. If you get just enough of it right, Amazon may list it in your chosen category when you first release the book, a few people buy it and then Amazon figures out it is in the right category and being shown among related books, simply because people are buying it from those pages.

A lot of this is guesswork which we can figure out by viewing and studying along with hundreds of hours of experimenting and browsing the Amazon store. We can just as easily find many examples of books that are selling well, which also have poor optimisation and relevancy. Most of the time this is because the book has managed to gather sales, possibly, although unlikely, because it got lucky. More often than not it is because the book was sold via advertising, the author already has at least some other books listed, has followers or many other possible reasons. Either way, relevancy will get your book shown in the right places. If you are a new author with no followers then this might be the very thing that will set you back if you don't pay attention to it.

Relevancy for Fiction

Making your book relevant with non-fiction is fairly straightforward as long as you pay attention to keywords and spend some time researching and experimenting with search results in Amazon. For fiction, things get trickier. To some extent you can only do so much. The problem with fiction is keywords are not so obvious and it's much harder to find them. Any that are obvious will be either very competitive, or will be in a genre of low interest. This doesn't mean you can't find keywords that perform well, they will just be much harder to find and will probably require a lot of hard work and experimenting through trial and error.

I should make it clear before I continue: I do not have any real world experience with selling fiction books on Amazon. I personally read very little fiction and don't have much interest in it. However, I do have many years experience with advertising and selling products on Amazon and eBay, as well as mail-order, my own websites and brick-and-mortar stores. What I write about in this section isn't pure guesswork. For the purpose of this book I have read and researched a lot of information about selling non-fiction. I have trawled through many forum / social media discussions and many hours of experimenting with Amazon search to get a feel for it. The conclusion is this: Selling fiction is no different from selling anything else on Amazon, with one major difference; keywords are harder to find and more trial and error will be required.

There is no easy answer to this. You can use keyword generators such as KDP Rocket to find ideas. These tools can be helpful but need to be used with some caution. Your book and the keywords you use must remain relevant to the book subject and genre. If you just grab as many keywords as you can without thinking carefully about them, then you run the risk of diminishing relevancy. Nothing is guaranteed with Amazon. You may find many books in the search results that contradict relevancy, don't let this be a reason for you to think it does not matter. If you are an unknown author without a following, then it matters.

If you are already getting sales on your books then you can probably worry less about being hyper-relevant. If you get sales, your rank increases and Amazon will figure out the type of readers that might like your book. If you are not getting any sales, nor showing up in the relevant categories and search results then it's possible that Amazon has tried to figure out your book, given up and thrown it in the sandpit.

If you are not getting any sales on your book then you should experiment with different keywords and make sure you are listed in the appropriate categories. If you have tried that and it's still not working then you will need to start thinking smarter and using different ideas. Advertising is obviously a good choice. You can also try making your book free and use countdown deals if you are enrolled in KDP Select. This can give you more chance of visibility and get some momentum going.

If your book is not yet released then it is worth spending a good amount of time thinking about categories and keywords before you publish it. Let's say it's a psychological thriller. You should search on Amazon for "psychological thriller" and look at the results. Take note of the categories that show up:

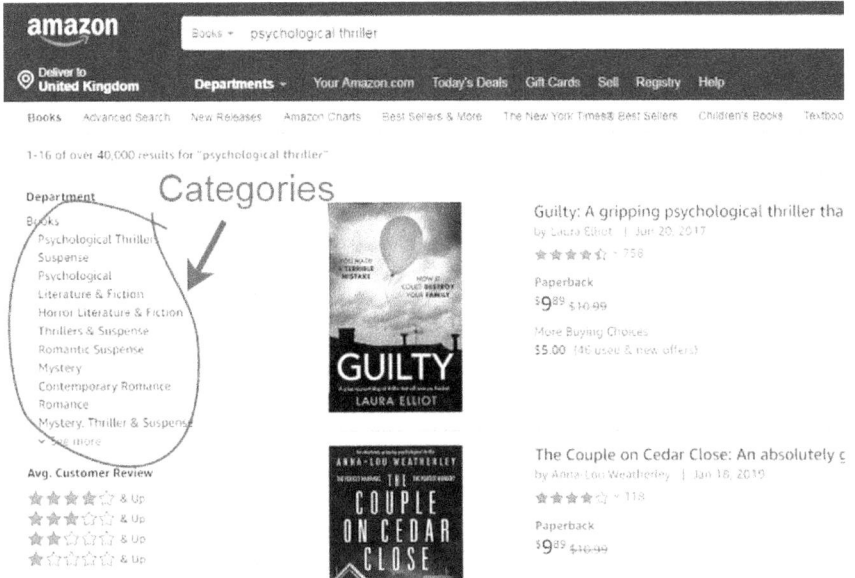

Write down the categories that you think most fit your book. Also search through the results and look for books that you think are similar, click through to those book pages and look at the categories they are listed in:

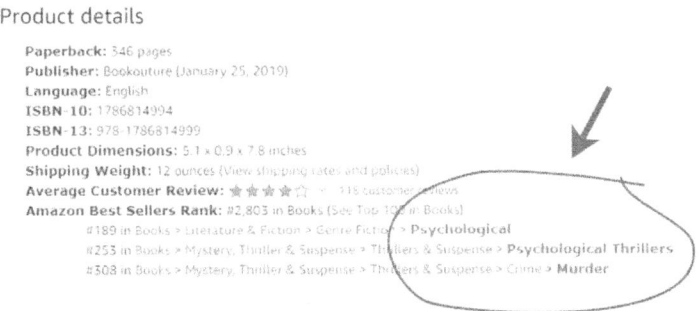

Don't try to copy the categories that other books are appearing in unless they are relevant. For instance, if your book is not about a murder then don't try to get into the "Murder" category, regardless of whether or not the books you research fit these categories. This may work for high ranking authors but doesn't mean it will for you if you aren't selling much. Amazon may put your book in non-relevant categories beyond your control, but try not to give them more reason to do so. Of course, it may just be that Amazon knows that all psychological thrillers sell well in the Murder category. There are times when the categories don't make sense (see chapter "running and optimising your ads") but avoid trying to influence this yourself unless you know for certain that it will be a good fit.

With non-fiction books it is easy for us to know where a book belongs. It's also quite easy for a computer algorithm to figure this out because the book, description, title, subtitle and the book's content will very likely have repetition of common keywords and phrases. For example, take a look at the words below and see if you can guess what the book is about?

Work for yourself
Be your own boss
Earn money
Start up
Small business
Entrepreneurship
Market research
Quit your day job
Paying taxes
Bookkeeping

Just from the first keyword phrase alone, I'm sure you guessed immediately that this book is all about working for yourself and the skills required for starting up a business. This is obvious, even to a computer algorithm. This is not because a computer is an all-knowing magical being; it's because it has been programmed to recognise these kinds of keywords.

Now look at the next list of words and decide what the book is about?

Boss
Detective
Agency
Entrepreneur
Murder
Research
Investigate
Money
Millionaire
Pathologist
Evidence

Okay, it's a fairly limited list of words but you could be reasonably confident that it's either a detective murder mystery involving a millionaire boss, or possibly it's a non-fiction book about starting up your own detective agency. However, it could be a true story about a documented murder. If so, is the focus on the murder case or is it all about the detective? If I threw in the words "how to" at the beginning then you'd be more inclined to guess "starting your own detective agency". If however it is fiction, is it serious or humour? Is it a romance novel about a relationship between a detective and pathologist? We can take guesses, but we cannot be certain. For a computer algorithm, this can be close to impossible. This is why we need to carefully use keywords and appropriate categories to guide the algorithms so that our book shows up in the right places.

If you browse through books in the bestseller categories and check various search results, you will often find books that don't really belong. It's almost certain that Amazon is having some difficulty figuring out exactly where the book should be seen because of some variation of the above example. How much is this a problem? I think it depends. You can often find high ranking bestsellers that aren't in the most appropriate categories, and occasionally listed in categories that are completely wrong. It clearly isn't that big a problem if the book's still making the bestseller list. The trouble is, we don't really know why some books show up in the wrong place. It could be because Amazon has figured out it sells well in certain areas, regardless of relevance. The most probable reason, however, is either because Amazon can't determine what the book is about based on the keywords, or the author has used incorrect, conflicting or vague information when setting up the book.

Some authors have a very broad audience. Take something like Harry Potter in it's heyday: it would have probably sold in a shoe shop. Bestselling authors with a big following are often searched for by author name or book title. If most Amazon sales come in from these kinds of searches or from links in newsletters and other websites, then the algorithms don't have anything to learn from as far as search keywords are concerned.

What we need to take from this is that if we aren't well known then nobody is searching for us or our book titles. Our sales will need to come from being shown in the correct places and relevant keyword searches that people are looking for. Not every reader is looking for a specific book title. These are the people we need to reach. If they are looking for a murder mystery and Amazon thinks our book is romance, then we have a problem.

This is why categories are so important for fiction. The book title and subtitle hold a lot of weight with keyword searches. This is great for non-fiction, not so good for fiction. You aren't going to title your book "Murder Mystery Novel". You could of course if you wanted to, but it doesn't sound very compelling. Even if you did, the higher ranking books in that category would bury it.

Best use of your time

Everything has a trade off. If you have a fascination for comparing numbers and studying graphs for hours on end then you are making good use of your time. For those of us that enjoy such strange activities, it is our mental challenge. No different from somebody who spends hours every day doing crosswords or playing Sudoku. If however, this stuff is just not your thing then don't get too hung up on it. Just get an overall feel for the basics and then accept being average at it, or even below average, just don't be bad at it. Here's the thing . ..

You could have the perfect book with perfect keywords, cover and description, get shown in all the right places and have highly relevant ad campaigns running, yet still get outsold by a book that is barely average at all of those things. It happens. "Selling" is a reasonably predictable science but it's not exact. Some things take you by surprise. You do however have to be somewhere in the ballpark. If you take no care over anything then you will probably be forever on a downward slope. For instance, let's imagine you write a book and do absolutely everything wrong. Terrible cover, wrong keywords, bad title and a five word description that just says "must read great suspense novel". No effort applied whatsoever. You are simply not going to sell books, no matter how many you publish. OK, you might sell a bare few but those sales would probably do you more harm than good with bad reviews and refunds which will harm your overall reputation among readers and Amazon author ranking.

Now compare that with two other books. One which you spend countless hours getting everything perfect and one which you apply all the basics, as best as you can without spending much time or effort. All three books we'll call Poor, Average and Perfect.

The Average book does not lie somewhere in the middle of effort vs sales. Average will be far better than poor.

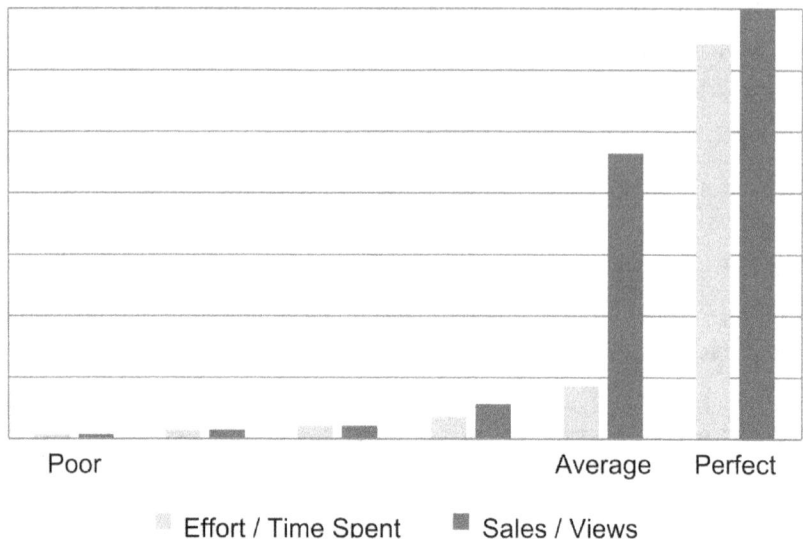

Poor   Average   Perfect

Effort / Time Spent   Sales / Views

I've not included any numbers in the chart above because it is hypothetical. Just use it as a visual representation of diminishing returns. You need to find the balance between what works and what is worth the effort. If you have no interest in something then your mind will burn out quickly. For example, I spend countless hours experimenting with Amazon search results and comparing advertising / sales charts. In the same amount of hours I could probably write and publish another two books per year. If I spend just enough time on those books trying to get an average balance of the right keywords, category placement etc., and then throw up some AMS ads that are generally in line with what I think should work, it might add up to a few hours per book. The sales on these new books will very likely exceed the extra sales I gain from countless hours of refining the books and adverts that I already have running. So why do I bother? Simply because I find it interesting. I also get bored if I do too much of the same thing. When I'm burned out with writing, I might do this instead. If you are the kind of person that can write endlessly, then that might be where the bulk of your effort should go.

The details cannot be ignored completely but once you have an understanding of how and where Amazon shows your book, just try to get it somewhat right and then carry on writing. If your books do not sell at all, perhaps then you can spend more time trying to figure out why.

Writing and publishing more books will nearly always trump spending too much time with details. Some things flop and we don't need to know why unless it becomes a common problem, in which case, the issues might lie beyond what we have looked at so far. Good keywords and categories will help get our books seen on Amazon. Things don't stop there unfortunately, we now need to convince the reader with the book's title, attractive cover and compelling description.

You Got Seen - Now What?

What we have looked at so far is trying to gain visibility on Amazon, hopefully in front of the right audience. If we can achieve that, we are over the first hurdle. It doesn't mean everyone will click on our book in the search results and look at the detail page. Something needs to catch their attention to make them want to click through to your book. A typical search results page doesn't show much, the most prominent being the cover, title and subtitle. For example, this is what we might see when we search for "murder mystery suspense novels".

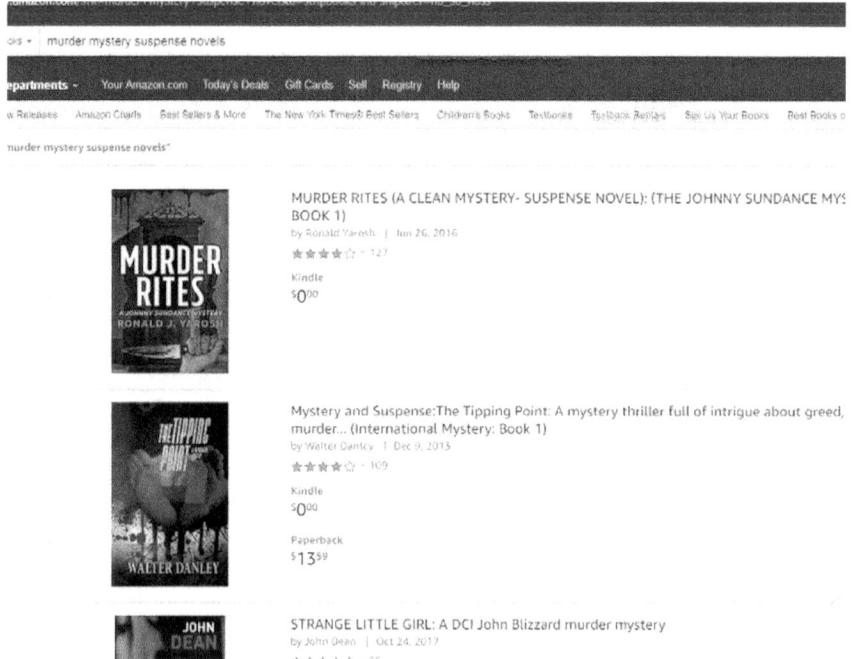

Your book might also get shown on other books detail pages among the "Also-boughts" or Sponsored products, as shown in the image below.

Customers who bought this item also bought

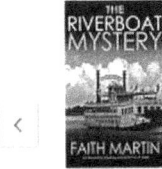

THE RIVERBOAT MYSTERY
an absolutely gripping
whodunit full of twists
FAITH MARTIN
★★★★☆ 40
Kindle Edition
$2.64

THE WINTER MYSTERY an
absolutely gripping
whodunit full of twists
FAITH MARTIN
★★★★☆ 110
Kindle Edition
$2.64

THE BIRTHDAY MYSTERY
an absolutely gripping
whodunit full of twists
FAITH MARTIN
★★★★☆ 107
Kindle Edition
$1.32

Murder at the Old House
A gripping and
unputdownable cozy...
Betty Rowlands
★★★★½ 16
Kindle Edition
$2.64

Sponsored products related to this item

A Bad, Bad Thing: a
psychological thriller
V. J. Chambers
A gripping and twisty
thriller. Would you help to...

THE RIVERBOAT MYSTERY
an absolutely gripping
whodunit full of twists
FAITH MARTIN

The Haunting of Abram
Mansion: A Riveting
Haunted House Mystery
Alexandria Clarke

Witches of The Wood: 7
Cozy Witch Mystery
Skylar Finn
When Samantha convince

Sometimes, Amazon will show similar books among "Customers also viewed ..." and "Recommended books", etc., and all of these things change over time. In all cases, much like the search results pages, you only see what is limited to pretty much the cover and title. Sponsored ads might also show Ad copy but we'll get to that later when we look at Amazon advertising.

At this point your only goal is to get someone to click on your book to read the description and possibly the reviews if you have any. This is where we need to think more like a marketer than an author, and it's not necessarily easy. The cover and title is what will make somebody choose to click on your book rather than somebody else's. Getting this to work well lies somewhere between science and luck. For non-fiction, it is much closer to science. For fiction, a little bit more luck perhaps but definitely not more luck than science. To get good at this stuff requires a lot of learning and experience. It cannot be taught in a few simple paragraphs and I certainly wouldn't claim to be an expert at it. What I can do is give you a basic understanding. For most of us it's all we need to know in order to be able to make an attempt at fixing things when they are not working, or improve things that are.

Marketers have been testing selling and advertising methods for many years and documenting the results. This is the science of selling. It's not guaranteed but if you stick to the principles you will succeed much more often than you fail. Sometimes things do not work even when everything is done right. On the other hand, things sometimes succeed when everything is done wrong or when the odds say otherwise. This is probably just luck; although this will likely become a science in time, it's just not fully understood yet. This is what we would call behavioural science and it's still in its infancy.

With non-fiction the science of selling is based quite heavily on logic, common sense and testing. With non-fiction the buyer / potential reader is searching for something based on either emotion, or something very specific like a particular book or author. Let's break these things down a little, starting with non-fiction.

Non-fiction is generally about something very specific. This could be anything from a puzzle book to self-help to learning how to do something. If you are looking for a book to help with anxiety, you will likely use fairly predictable or common search phrases. Things like:

How to cure anxiety.

Anxiety workbook
Help with anxiety
How to stop panic attacks
Anxiety self help

And so on. If we do a search for "stop panic attacks" we see something like this:

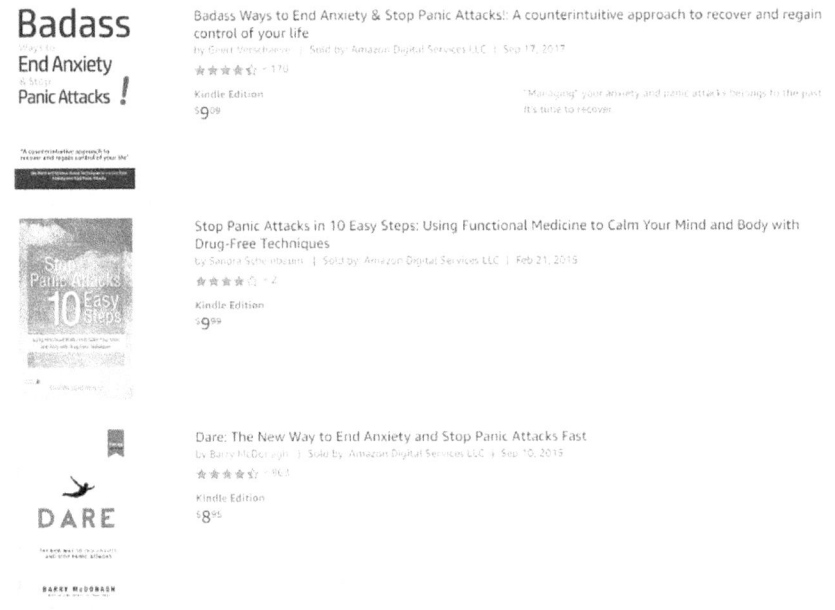

As you scroll down the search page, one of those books will grab your attention more than another. Most people will glance at the cover and then read the text, but more likely than not, it will be the title and subtitle that convinces you to click. For non-fiction, a pretty cover is not what we want. It certainly needs to look professional but, more importantly, it needs to convey the message. This is done most efficiently with large text on the cover, describing what you are searching for.

Look at the first book, "Badass ..." it jumps out at you, and with a momentary glance, you know exactly what this book is about, you'll probably scan your eyes immediately to the right and read the title, which is what's written on the book cover. The subtitle invokes a bit of curiosity, "A counterintuitive approach ..." this will probably make you think this book might be different to all the others you may have already read on the subject. Counterintuitive sounds potentially interesting and your curiosity might make you click to read more.

The second book down, is not such a good cover. The title is not bad, "Stop Panic Attacks in 10 easy Steps," sounds exactly like something we might be looking for. The main problem with it is the text blends into the background and so doesn't jump out like the first one, which has already grabbed most of your attention. The subtitle: "Using Functional Medicine ..." what even is that? It all sounds a bit too hippie and alternative to me. I feel pretty certain that this book would get more clicks if the cover was made much clearer and the subtitle either removed completely or altered to "Calm Your Mind and Body with these Simple Techniques"

The third book, "Dare". The subtitle is OK, it's what we are looking for. The title and the cover, not so good. My first thought when I look at this cover is a book for adrenaline junkies. The subtitle is small text, therefore difficult to read in a thumbnail image. If you look at the amount of reviews, it's obvious this book is selling well. This is more likely to do with the fact that the author is already quite a big name in anxiety and panic attacks. If this were our own book and we were unknown then this would unlikely be a good cover.

Here's the thing with marketplaces like Amazon. People tend to search for something, click on the first book or product that grabs their attention and then don't often click back to the initial search page. If they click on the Badass book, read the description and then decide it's not what they are looking for, most of the time they will navigate away from that page via the also-boughts or sponsored ads.

To sum up, non-fiction covers should stand out and be obvious with a title that is designed to grab attention. Copywriting techniques can be used to create a title that attracts interest. For instance, if you have a book about how to build a shed: try to make it specific. There would be nothing wrong with simply titling it "How to Build a Shed" which would be likely to get more clicks than a book called "Shed Design". Don't try to be clever with a non-fiction title. "How to Build a Shed out of Recycled Junk" will probably get more clicks than "Build a Beautiful Shed Using Reclaimed Materials".

I don't know for certain if the above would be true. My experience with selling says it's likely. We can however never be certain and that's why we should test things. Even if we preferred the latter title, we would still need to think about how people search for books on Amazon and as far as keywords are concerned, using the words "how to build a shed" within the title is going to cause no confusion to the search algorithms.

You should equip yourself with a basic understanding of copywriting principles. There are plenty of books and Internet articles that can help with this, so seek some out. Writing non-fiction book titles is no different from writing headlines designed to grab attention. One of my favourite books on copywriting is "Write to Sell" by Andy Maslen. It's not a difficult read and covers all of the principles involved for writing headlines and sales writing which is basically what we do with our book title and description.

Enough about titles, what about artwork and images on our book cover, do they play a big part in grabbing attention? I think the answer to this is yes, no and maybe. The best way to figure this out is to just look at the bestsellers in your category. A lot of bestselling non-fiction books do not benefit from having a picture on the cover. To some extent they may even cause a distraction or do more harm than good. Many self-help books, for example, do not have pictures on the cover, just often a few colours to break things up a bit. However, a book about building sheds would probably benefit from an image of a shed because it instantly tells us "this is a book about sheds".

Either way, book covers are best left to professionals that know what they are doing. You should still research similar books to yours to get a feel for what the typical bestselling covers look like so that you can tell your designer the type of thing you are looking for. Pictures and artwork should not be a distraction for the book title, which must stand out clearly at all costs.

So what about fiction books? This one is a difficult subject. The same principles apply, the cover, title and subtitle (if you use one) all need to grab attention and give the reader (potential buyer) an instant impression that this is the kind of book they are looking for. The problem here is we have no logical approach to build on. The cover image is far more important for fiction, it needs to say something about the book, even more so if you are an unknown author. There is no harm in checking out the types of cover used by other books in your genre but this is without doubt an area best left to professionals.

The title is just as difficult. It needs to attract interest but we can't easily use any copywriting techniques, other than perhaps in the subtitle. A search on Amazon for "murder mystery" shows results of quite a few books with subtitles like "A Gripping Mystery full of Twists". Some of these are high ranking books so this is perhaps the only place we can do something obvious. The main title, however will be fully dependant on the story so only you can decide what's best for that. If you can make it somehow intriguing then do so, but don't allow it to detract from the story.

You got Clicked - Now What?

The goal of everything so far has been to try getting people to your book's detail page. This is the page where people can read your book description, read the reviews and use the "Look Inside" feature. This is the place where we have to try to convince people to buy our book and it can be the difference between make or break. Reviews can help or hinder our book sales, unfortunately we can't do anything about them so hopefully they will be mostly positive. Negative reviews will always happen, no matter how good the book is. All we can do is try to keep them to a minimum so it's important to make sure the book title and description are accurate and honest.

For non-fiction, if you over-hype everything in the description just to attract sales, you will ultimately get more bad reviews. Just make sure your book does offer what it promises. Fiction is similar but the descriptions are written entirely different as they are more about story telling than fact giving. I'm not going to attempt to give any advice on writing descriptions for fiction books, this is best left to those who know a lot more about it than I do. Either way, you should try to educate yourself on the basics. Two popular books on this very subject are:

Brian Meeks: Mastering Amazon Descriptions
Bryan Cohen: How to Write a Sizzling Synopsis

I've not read them myself but I hear good things about them so probably worth checking out. Copywriting techniques are still used to an extent with fiction. For example, within the book description you might see things like; "An Amazon Bestseller" or "an action packed thriller that will keep you on the edge of your seat" ... and so on. You will also see testimonial quotes sometimes included at the bottom of the description. Do these things work for fiction? I'd guess they probably do because you will find many bestselling authors using them. I would say be careful with them. Certainly don't make them up. If you use testimonials then make sure they are genuine. Also, make sure you keep up to date with Amazon's terms and conditions. They change frequently and just because you see others doing it, doesn't mean they aren't necessarily breaking Amazon's terms.

Non-fiction descriptions rely on typical copywriting principles and you should take some time to learn the basics. This is not a book on copywriting but let's take a look at a few things you should think about.

Descriptions are a sales pitch. We use this space to convince somebody that this is the book for them. Let's say our book is about learning how to play the piano. We could write something like this:

Learn essential piano skills and practice routines. No experience required, become the pianist you always dreamed of.

It's short, it's boring and it doesn't tell us much. It might get a few sales but most people will move on and look at other books pretty quickly. Potential buyers of "How to" books are often looking for something quite specific. Sometimes they need to be reminded of what those specifics actually are. Let's try again:

Learn how to play piano the easy way.
Ideal for beginners. Anybody can learn how to play the piano with this easy to follow method.
No music reading skills required ... includes over 100 diagrams that show you exactly where to put your fingers!
Learn common piano chords that you can use to play all of your favourite songs. This book will show you how.

This is a bit better. The first line tells us straight away that it will be showing us an easy way. We all like things that are easy, right? The rest of it addresses a few of the questions the reader might have: *ideal for beginners, anybody can do it;* If we've never played piano before, we now know this book is suitable for us. No need to learn to read music, great! Diagrams show us where to put our fingers and we can learn to play the chords to our favourite songs.

Overall, this is still quite short but it isn't bad. It's likely to get a few more people buying the book with this description rather than the first shorter one. Could we do better than this? Probably. Copywriting is a skill that takes time to learn. Many of us don't have the time to learn and gain the experience necessary to become experts in this field, nor do we all have the money to pay professionals. Remember, we should make best use of our time. In the time it takes to master copywriting skills, we could put that effort into getting more books written and published. If, however, we learn some basics and do the best we can with them, we'll get better each time we do it.

There are a few golden rules and tips for writing sales copy. Here are the four most important ones.

1. Grab their attention.
2. People are not interested in you, only themselves.
3. Write more about benefits, less about features.
4. Write as though you are talking to one person.

Let's take a look at each one. We start by getting their attention. This is the very first line and its only job is to make them want to read more. Headlines have been tested (for many years) and proven to work with certain trigger words. Among some of the most common are headlines that start with the following:

- Finally
- Introducing
- How to
- Who else

We could use these something like this:

Finally, a piano teaching method that actually works
Introducing a brand new piano learning system that will have you
playing in half the time
How to play the piano, from scratch, in 30 days or less!
Who else wants to learn to play the piano with a system so simple, your
3 year old could do it?

Notice how they all sound a bit bullshitty? Unfortunately these kinds of headlines still work. I personally wouldn't use them unless they are based on some reality. The headline does need some kind of qualifier though. For example:

How to play the piano
How to play the piano, from scratch, in 30 days or less!

The shorter one won't grab as much attention. The more outrageous, the better, but be careful because people are becoming desensitised to these types of headlines. You could change this to sound a bit more honest, something like ...

How to play the piano, from scratch, with this easy to follow system.

It's more truthful but lacks a bit of punch. We could perhaps try adding a bit of curiosity to it ...

How to play the piano, from scratch, with "revolutionary" new system

Quotes are used around the word "revolutionary" to make it stand out. You could also make it stand out by using all upper case or underline it. All of these ideas can work, you just need to decide how much you are prepared to over-hype things. I personally prefer to think long term: I want my readers coming back for my other books, so I will try to use something a bit punchy if possible, but also credible.

No 2: People are not interested in you. For example:

I have played piano for over twenty years. My first year of piano lessons felt like I didn't achieve anything. I wanted to play the piano badly but got to the point where I was wondering if I was just kidding myself. Luckily I stuck with it and become a professional pianist and music teacher.

The good thing about teaching others is it has given me the ability to figure out why I had so much trouble for the first couple of years. Turns out it wasn't me that was the problem, it was the teaching methods. I now use a completely different approach with my students and my method is outlined in this book. I will show you how to play the piano and get fast results with my piano learning system.

It's a common mistake to think that by explaining your struggles, people will relate to your pain and assume you know what you are talking about, therefore can help them with the same problems. While this is true, the focus needs to be mostly on the reader, not you. There is nothing wrong with telling your story and how you overcame it, especially if it relates to the same struggles the reader is likely going through. In fact it can be quite powerful but just be careful not to overdo it and make sure it gets straight to the point.

No 3: More about benefits, less about features.

Features are what your product does or includes. Benefits are what your product can do for the person looking to buy your product.

Includes Chord Diagrams is a feature.
Includes audio examples is a feature.

Easy to follow is a benefit.
Learn in your own time is a benefit.
Less practice required is a benefit.

Writing about a feature is fine, but the benefits of that feature is what's important. You can combine the two.

Includes over 50 chord diagrams, each one clearly showing you exactly where to put your fingers. You don't even need to know how to read music!

Audio examples are included so you can hear every example as it should sound. No more confusion, it's like having a teacher sitting right beside you.

It's straightforward enough. Describe a feature and explain why it's good for them. Avoid over-describing. People get bored quickly and don't need to know every detail. The following is far too much and not necessary.

Includes over 50 diagrams, each one photographed in a professional studio with a carefully angled camera allowing you to see exactly where to put your fingers on the piano keyboard. Reading music is complicated and takes a long while to learn, fortunately no music reading skills are required with my system.

I will already assume that the diagrams were made in such a way that I can read them clearly. The details are of no interest to me, I'm already bored. Also, I can already guess that music reading is complicated, I've seen the squiggly lines, it looks like hell. Do I need to know how to read music? No? That's all that matters to me.

No 4: Talk to one person.

Don't write this:
Thousands of people wish they could play the piano but think it's too difficult. Now anybody can learn how to play with my easy piano learning method.

Write this:
So you want to play the piano? Well, it just got easy. "Title of book" takes the misery out of learning with this fast, easy to follow method that will have you playing in no time.

Use the title of the book where it makes sense. If it doesn't then you could write something like: My *method takes the misery out ...* etc.

OK, all of that is the general idea. Now we should decide exactly what the book is about and talk straight to that person. Not everyone will want your book, don't try selling to those that won't be interested. In this case, the book is aimed at people that want to play piano and would like to get good at it but not trying to be a concert pianist. Those that want to jam with friends, play in a local band and not want it to be any more difficult than necessary. Let's see if we can use these ideas to improve our book description.

Learn How to Play Piano, from Scratch, the Easy Way

So you want to play piano but it just feels like too much effort? Not any more ... Piano just got easy.
It took me well over a year to show any progress when I first started. You can do it much quicker. Here's why ...

Most teachers work from the ground up. Every boring detail, repeated over and over, one tiny step at a time. It's not fun, it's torture. You don't want that, I didn't want that. I, like you, wanted to play songs, jam with friends and other musicians and just have fun. Here's the thing ...

Formal, and common, teaching methods are designed to train you slowly, preparing you to be at the top of your game. That's a lot of wasted effort for most of us. It's like training to be an athlete, 90% more work and practice to knock one second off of their track time.

This book cuts out that 90% extra effort and gets you straight into learning the things that will have you playing competently, in the shortest time possible.

It includes all of the popular chords that will have you playing your favourite songs fast, with easy to follow practice routines that concentrate on getting you there quickly, with no wasted effort.

- *No music reading skills required.*
- *Over 60 diagrams that show you exactly where to put your fingers*
- *Includes the common scales that you need to jam along with almost any song.*
- *Audio examples for each lesson so that you can hear exactly how it should sound. It's like having your very own teacher sitting beside you.*

Don't waste any more time, get this book now and you'll be immediately on your way to playing the piano like you've always dreamed of.

OK, there's a bit of hype there, but we need to have a little bit because it works. As long as it's not too far fetched or obvious nonsense that will end up getting you bad reviews then all should be OK. I could try giving it more hype or possibly cut it back a bit and then test it out. If sales don't seem as good as they should be, I would probably try changing it a little bit at a time and then test for another week or two.

The main goal with writing book descriptions is to keep the reader interested enough to read through all of it and not give up after the first few lines. I feel like I've added some interesting stuff in there. Also note, that the whole thing is broken up into small paragraphs. This makes it easier to read on computer screens and tablets etc. Also note that the first two paragraphs end with something like "here's why ...". It adds some curiosity to make them want to read on.

The last line is a call to action telling them to buy it now. These kind of prompts can be surprisingly effective. Just remember to keep an eye on Amazon's terms and conditions if you say things like "scroll up and click the buy button". There might come a time when what you include in your book description today, will become against their terms in the future.

Will this book description work much better than the first two attempts? Probably, but not definitely. Never assume that because you have done things the recommended way it will be guaranteed to work. Just understand the principles, try your best, and if it doesn't work, refine it, or if necessary, try something else. As the old saying goes: "if at first you don't succeed, try again".

Small Things Add Up

A lot of what we have looked at so far can make a big difference. A great book cover can stand out and grab far more attention than a poor one. The result is more clicks, more people looking at your book's detail page. A title like "Piano Learning Guide" is almost certain to get fewer clicks than "How to Play Piano the Easy Way".

Some things make small differences and we can't always predict them. Two titles with subtle differences are more likely to have closely matched results. For example:

"How to Play Piano the Easy Way"
"Learn How to Play Piano, Easily"

What one will do better? We won't really know unless we try them both. Unfortunately it's not always a good idea to change a book's title as it will probably require a new ISBN and change of cover. Unless your book flops completely, this is best left alone.

The cover, keywords metadata and description can be changed whenever you like. Always check before doing so however, just in case Amazon's terms change.

When you make changes, only ever do one change at a time and let it run for a few weeks. If you don't then you'll have no idea what is working and what isn't.

When we make changes, the results might be small but collectively they can make a big difference. Let's look at some easy to follow hypothetical numbers for our learn piano book. Assume we've named it "How to play the piano".

We'll assume this gets about 1000 impressions in the search results everyday and gets 1 click in a thousand. We'll also assume that the book makes a sale for every 20 clicks, so we need the book to show up 20,000 times to make one sale, that's one sale every twenty days.

Everything so far is quite generic, we haven't put much thought into the keywords or description, let's say we're using the second description discussed in the last section. If we change the description to the more hyped one and let it run for a few weeks we might see that our clicks to sales increase from 1 in 20 to 1 in 17. This means our sales will jump from one every twenty days to one every 17 days. Don't sound much? Don't worry.

After a few weeks testing, we try a different book cover and find the click rate jumps a bit higher. It now takes 900 impressions to get a click instead of 1000. So far this means we have gone from needing 20,000 impressions to make one sale, down to 15,300.

We can also assume that the longer description has helped us show up in search results for a few more keywords, let's say that has picked up up an extra 150 impressions per day. This doesn't change our click through rate but it does mean that every six days we get an extra click. Now we'll do some research and use Amazon search suggestions and look at other high ranking books to see if we can find some good keywords to use in our book details (7 keyword fields) in KPD settings. We can use keywords phrases and multiple keywords in each of the seven boxes. For this hypothetical example, let's say I've done my research and found seven good keyword phrases that relate to my book are:

1: Piano for beginners
2: Piano scales
3: Piano chords

4: Learn to play jazz piano
5: Piano lessons
6: Learn blues piano
7: Boogie woogie piano

Amazon suggest we should use phrases that people are likely to type into the search box and not to repeat words already used in our title. I've got no reason to believe otherwise but if you can't think of anything else then just use common search suggestions. We could try single words that are not used in our title but I'll use phrases which are searched for and not worry about reusing words like "piano", I'll use complete phrases.

We now have a good chance of getting more impressions for other keyword searches. Also, these changes are giving Amazon algorithms more information so that it has a better idea of what our book is about. Whenever we make changes, the effects aren't instant and may take days or weeks to notice the difference.

Once everything has settled we might now find that our book is showing up in search results 2000 times per day, getting a click for every 900 impressions (possibly more now that we are attracting different search phrases) and we have increased our sales rate from 1 in 20 to 1 in 17 clicks. The result is this: from 1 sale every 20 days, to approximately 2 sales every 15 days.

It might not seem like a lot but remember, we're only talking about how small changes can add up. The reality is if you have a book with a poor title, cover, description and bad choice of keywords, these differences won't be small, they will be huge. You might find you go from hardly any sales at all - to selling two books per day, maybe twenty, maybe more. It can be literally make or break.

Sales Rank

Keywords, book titles and everything discussed so far about optimising your book details will add weight to your search potential and click through rate. However, nothing adds as much weight as sales rank. Every time you make a sale, your book's potential for showing up in search or on other book's pages increases significantly. The problem is, however, that this potential moves in either direction with every sale.

Nobody really knows how Amazon uses sales rank but what we do know is this. The more a book sells, the higher the rank; the higher the rank, the more our book will show up to potential buyers. Amazon sells probably hundreds of thousands of books per day, which means that every time somebody else makes a sale, and we don't, our rank decreases again because we get knocked out of our position.

Note: High rank is a lower number, it refers to the selling position, i.e., the book ranked #1 is the number 1 bestseller. If you are ranked at #100,000 then you are the 100,000th bestselling book. This is updated hourly (as far as I know) so with many thousands of books selling daily, your sales rank will drop very quickly if you only make one sale in a day.

There is speculation that sales rank over time will add weight to our book's search potential. I suspect this is correct. There is no point in getting hung up about sales rank or paying much attention to it. The only thing that moves sales rank is sales, and borrows if you are in Kindle Unlimited, so the only thing we need to worry about is trying to get sales.

If you are getting no sales whatsoever then it's probable that as your rank moves increasingly lower, it will end up gathering virtual dust as Amazon will consider it a non-seller and show it less in the search results. As long as you get at least one or two sales per week, I don't think this is something worth worrying about.

One thing that sales rank is good for is giving us some hope. Earlier I was talking about the amount of competition we are up against with the millions of books sold on Amazon. What sales rank can show us is that this competition isn't quite so big as it appears. Here's why; if you release a new book and make just one sale, your rank will immediately be a few hundred thousand. This tells us that our competition is in the hundreds of thousands, not millions. Not forgetting that this competition is for the top spot among all book categories. If we take a look at something like the piano category for our example book, the 100th bestselling book is (currently) ranked at 303,000. This means that for our category, one or two sales might be all we need to get into the top 100. It won't make us suddenly rich, but seeing it in this light gives us a lot more hope.

Amazon Advertising

When all else fails, there's Amazon Advertising, formerly known as AMS (Amazon Marketing Services). Unfortunately it is slowly becoming a necessary evil. Before AMS was introduced, other than promoting from outside of Amazon, we only had optimisation to worry about, i.e., the things discussed so far in this book. This used to work quite well on it's own, but things were different then: there was a lot less competition. Now we have to pay for the privilege of getting noticed.

Whether we like it or not, this is how things are. I don't like it personally, but for different reasons than most: it's an expensive playground for people who don't understand the system ... who are forced to play.

The thing is, nobody can be blamed for struggling to understand Amazon Advertising (or any digital advertising system, they all work similarly). It's a whole new ball-game compared to traditional advertising and it can get very expensive, very quickly. It's complicated. The best way to get your head around it is to start with what we already know, and work backwards.

Traditional advertising was pretty straightforward. We had a product or service, we placed an advertisement in a periodical such as a magazine or newspaper etc., and hopefully it got some attention and created sales. Generally speaking, how much we pay for the advert depends on the size of readership, the placement, the available space and the ad size.

Placement in periodicals and newspapers would be priced at where you want your ad to appear. Cost would vary from top of page, bottom, middle, left, right, first page, last page, somewhere in the middle, column size and so on. It's all about "eyeballs".

More people will see your ad at the top of the page because that's where people look first, so you pay more for that spot. A lot of readers never, or rarely look at the last few pages and so on.

If you are advertising your product in a very popular newspaper then it needs to be something that sells to a broad audience. Let's say for instance you are selling fishing rods: the back pages of a newspaper is probably not going to be the best place for you to advertise. Imagine a newspaper with 1 million daily readers. Only 30% (hypothetical numbers here) of those readers bother to read the back pages and only 50% of those actually notice your ad. Of those people, only 5% are actually interested in fishing and 80% of them are not looking to buy a new fishing rod. Sounds crazy but it's how you need to think when spending your money on advertising.

So with 1 million readers, 30% that look at the back is 300,000. 50% actually notice the ad, we're down to 150,000. 5% interest in fishing = 7500 and 20% might possibly be persuaded to buy a new fishing rod = 1500. That's a newspaper with 1m readers that you are hoping for 1500 of them to not only spot your ad, but also read it and be persuaded. The problem here is relevancy. It's surprising how many people do not understand this until they have wasted a lot of money. Trust me, I've been there, done that. We can easily get caught in the trap of not fully understanding the importance of this. A million readers means nothing if hardly any of them are interested. Advertising your book on Amazon in the incorrect category is similar to this.

Relevancy is about cost efficiency. I have no idea how many fishing rods you could sell from a newspaper ad, it might be surprisingly high. The problem is it's an expensive experiment. Fine if you have money to play with. People buy newspapers to read news, not adverts. Don't get fooled by the large number of readers.

Obviously if we were selling a fishing rod then we wouldn't necessarily be looking to advertise in a generic newspaper, there are plenty of magazines that specialise in fishing, we'd advertise there right? Yes we would but what if it only had 75,000 readers and the advertisement cost was actually more than the newspaper with 1m readers? This is where it can all go wrong for us: many people will reconsider the newspaper option in this case. Again, it's all about relevancy. How much is each reader actually worth?

The people buying the fishing magazine are all interested in fishing rods. Not necessarily looking to buy one right now but all have an interest nevertheless. Depending on how good your ad copy is, you may even be able to convince those who are not ready to buy. The other thing about specialist magazines is people often look through them multiple times so you get more than one opportunity for them to notice and read your ad. Readers of specialist magazines also have a much higher percentage of people that read right through, or at least browse through all of the pages. It don't take a genius to work out that you will probably sell more fishing rods from advertising in a dedicated fishing magazine than you would from a throw away newspaper with a very broad audience. The problem with Amazon Advertising is so many people are doing this very thing, they just don't realise it. It's much harder to spot the obvious.

The Feedback Loop

Now imagine this. The fishing magazine that you have been advertising in calls you up one day and says "we've had a change of rules regarding our advertising". "We now do call forwarding and you will be required to use a unique phone number in your advert, which we will provide, and then forward all your calls". They then monitor this number to see how many calls you get from your advert. Using this information, they count the amount of calls your ad receives and compare it with other advertisers. If another advertiser with a similar advert gets more calls than you then they will give that advert more priority over yours in the next publication. You get pushed out of your spot and moved further to the back of the magazine. You can get your spot back but you'll have to pay more.

This starts a bidding war. You pay more, but so does the other advertiser. If that isn't bad enough, you get another call. "We're now requiring all advertisers to use our ordering system". The calls are no longer forwarded, the magazine takes the call, takes the order and then forwards you the customer's details. This now gets monitored. The amount of calls are now weighed up against the amount of orders to decide where you will be placed in the magazine. You can get your spot back but you will need to pay even more, or make sure your ad is performing well. We can call this the placement algorithm.

All of this is a very crude analogy of how the Amazon algorithms do their thing. The big difference is that it's all in real time, very dynamic and many other factors are included and counted towards how much you pay, and where you will get seen.

Not many people would bother to advertise a fishing rod in a magazine all about knitting, but let's suppose we did. Using the same criteria as above, all advertisers that are doing better than ours will get better positioning and pay less for the same spot. Our ad will be extremely unlikely to get many, if any, calls or sales so we will be quickly pushed to the back pages. Because low sales and calls are weighted against our advert, price alone might never be enough to get us anywhere near the front or middle pages. Eventually we might get a call from the publisher saying they have decided to no longer run our ad.

In it's most basic form, this is pretty much how Amazon advertising works. The main difference is there are probably hundreds, maybe thousands of different criteria weighed in favour of, or against our ad placement and bid price. We'll never know what they all are, and even if we did, it wouldn't matter much as they get updated regularly. Paying attention to relevancy will be your biggest safeguard against your ads becoming either too expensive or failing all together.

Do we Need to Advertise?

I said earlier, advertising on Amazon is becoming a necessary evil. Unless you have a reasonable sized following, or promote outside of Amazon using some other method, then chances are you will need to face up to it. It's easy to get disheartened and believe that Amazon will stop at nothing to grab more money from you. While this is possibly true, understand it's just a reality of all business and affects everybody, not just authors. Selling books is a business whether you like it or not. Either you deal with the business side of things, or pay an agent to deal with it. Somebody has to do it.

You need to be realistic if you want to sell books. If you sell a product, then you are in business. If you are a business then you should think nothing of investing in it and not be frightened to take a gamble. If you are completely broke or do not have a job, then maybe you'll have to wait until your circumstances change, or try to get creative and find some other way. Advertising in the digital age can get expensive very quickly so be careful. The good part is that you can control your budget so it doesn't get out of hand. How much money do you need? It's hard to say. Personally I was prepared to gamble $500 on advertising for my first book just as an experiment and consider it my learning fee. Didn't really matter whether I lost it or not. Fortunately I didn't, but I do have experience with other advertising platforms, including Amazon Seller Central which is almost the same thing. What I did lack was experience with selling books, which was zero.

If you cannot afford to take a chance with at least $100 then, maybe rethink it, or at least first spend a lot of time studying and reading everything you can about it. The problem with very small budgets is that you just won't gather enough data to learn anything. It also doesn't give the algorithms enough time to figure things out. Advertising needs to be refined over time. You may start off making a loss, figure out where you are losing money, solve that problem and adjust things until they are working. You cannot do this with very small budgets but if you manage to keep losses small then you will be making money back from your book so it's not all bad.

Your ultimate goal is to profit from your ads but if you can get them to just break even, you are still in profit. Just in a different way. If you break even then you are potentially building an audience for free, don't underestimate the value of this. In the meantime you will be learning and collecting data that will help you improve over time.

In the next few sections we'll take a look at the basics of setting up and analysing advertising campaigns. It won't get too involved for two reasons. 1: it is extremely time consuming when you try too hard to reverse engineer the data, that time is probably better spent writing more books. 2: reverse engineering the Amazon algorithms is a fruitless task, it's just too random. There's also a third reason: if you do discover something, you can bet your life it won't last long.

Ad Types

At present, April 2019 while I'm writing this, there are Two Ad types.

- Sponsored Products
- Lockscreen Ads

Sponsored Products come in four variations.

- Automatic targeting
- Manual keyword targeting
- Manual category targeting
- Manual product targeting

Automatic targeting is the easiest. Amazon decides where to show the ad. This can show up in search results and book detail pages in the sponsored ad carousel.

Manual keyword targeting ads show up in search results when somebody types in search terms that you bid for. You can also get shown on related product detail pages among the sponsored ads. For example, if you use author names or book titles as keywords then you may show up on the page of those books.

Manual category ads will show your ad in the sponsored ad carousel on the detail pages of books listed in specific categories.

Manual product targeting ads will show up on specific book's pages that you choose.

Sponsored product ads can also show up as banner ads on detail pages. This is quite new and seems to have replaced what used to be display ads. So far it's hard to tell how or when these will appear, I think Amazon are still experimenting with them.

We'll go through these one by one a little later. From here on out, I'll probably refer to all of these ads simply as; Auto, keyword, category and product ads.

Lockscreen Ads are quite new and so far, I haven't heard of anybody having much luck with them. They are very straightforward, they show up on Kindle readers and Fire tablets when the screen is unlocked. The general consensus so far is ... they don't work for most people.

I'm not going to talk about setting them up because they are very similar to setting up Sponsored product category targeting.

Your Advertising Account

If you already have an advertising account and know how to setup the ads, you can skip this part.

If you have not yet setup your adverting account then you can do so from your KDP dashboard. Next to your book, from the edit button, click on Promote and Advertise. I can't quite remember the exact steps but here's what it says on the Amazon help page.

Create an Amazon Advertising account
1.Go to your Bookshelf.
2.Choose the live KDP book you want to advertise.
3.Click Promote and Advertise under KINDLE EBOOK ACTIONS or PAPERBACK ACTIONS.
4.Under "Run an Ad Campaign," click Create an Ad Campaign. If you haven't set up an Amazon Advertising account, this will create your account and sign you in.

This is what you are looking for ...

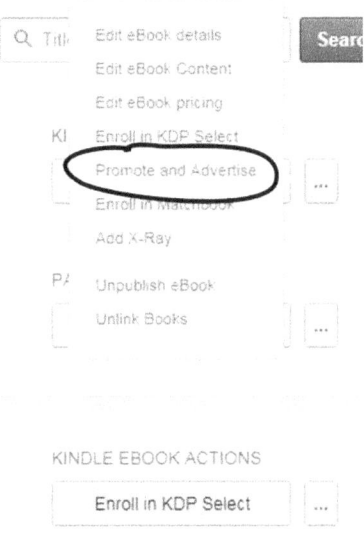

If you already have an account then just go to your advertising dashboard and click on the create campaign button to setup a new ad.

Clicking this button will bring you to a page where you choose your ad type. For all of the following ads we will be discussing, click on the Sponsored Products.

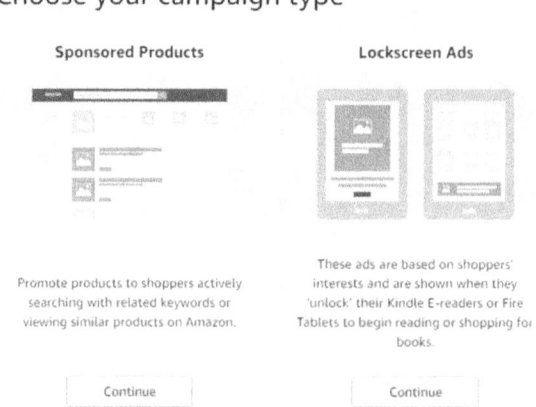

Sponsored Product Ads

Once you click on Sponsored Product, you will be taken to a page with a few options. At the top of the page you will see this.

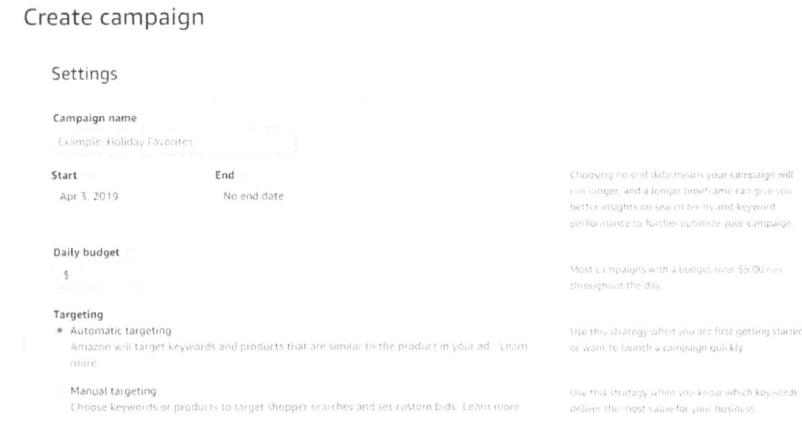

Here you can create the name for your campaign, start and end date, daily budget and targeting type.

Campaign name

Name it what makes sense to you but bear in mind that campaigns will always show up on your dashboard, even once they have ended. Over time, the more campaigns you create, the more of a mess the dashboard becomes. Personally I use the book name or some abbreviation of the book title and the campaign type or anything that makes it as logical as possible to me. If I have a book named "How to Play Piano" I may use something like "HTPP KW Optimised" or HTTP Auto. KW Optimised would tell me it's manual keyword targeting in which I use the best performing keywords only.

Start and end date

Set the start date for when you like, you'll most likely want to leave it at the current date so that it starts as soon as possible. The end date is always best left as no end date unless you know for certain that you want it to run for a set amount of time. You can change the end date afterwards but only while the campaign is running. If you have a campaign doing well, which you forget to keep an eye on ... once it's ended it cannot be started again. I've done this and killed a campaign that was doing well. If it's set to no end date, you can pause and restart the campaign whenever you like until you decide to end it manually.

Daily budget

You will get many opinions on this. Some say that setting a high budget will get you more impressions. I can't verify this and haven't personally seen any evidence of it but that's not to say it isn't working for others. Maybe it's possible in more competitive areas. Either way, go sensible if you are just starting out, maybe $5 or $10. If the campaign works well and runs out of budget, you can always change it after. Just remember to keep an eye on it.

Targeting

Choose manual or automatic targeting here. Depending on which one you choose, different options will appear further down the page for adding keywords.

Campaign bidding strategy

Bidding strategy can be quite confusing. So much so that we'll look at it in a later chapter.

Ad Format

As you scroll down the page, this is the next thing you should see.

Custom text ad is where you can enter your ad copy. "Standard ad" doesn't use any ad copy (more in this is a moment).

Products

Here you will see a list of your books. Choose the book you want to advertise and click the "Add" button.

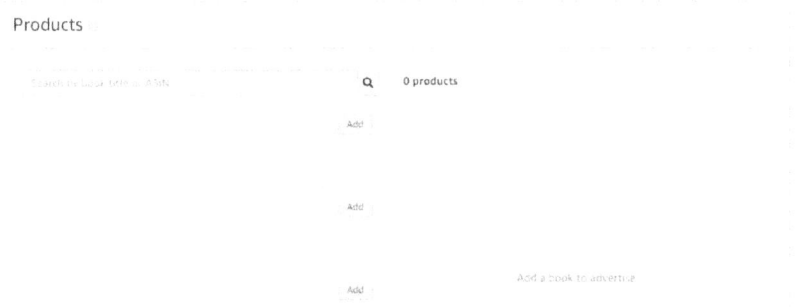

Automatic Targeting

If you chose automatic targeting earlier then here is where you can set your default bid price. For auto campaigns you will use a single bid price for the whole campaign. You can change it afterwards if you like, personally I would start lower, maybe 0.20 or 0.30 but that depends on how competitive I think the ad might be.

If you check the box which says "Set bids by targeting group" you will see an expanded section where you can set bids by targeting groups.

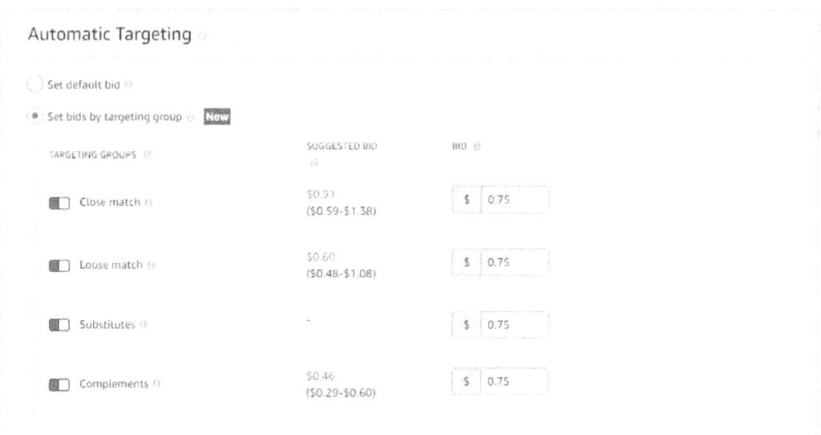

Amazon does not give much information about what these match types are other than the following.

- Close match: Amazon may show your ad to shoppers who use search terms closely related to your products
- Loose match: Amazon may show your ad to shoppers who use search terms loosely related to your products.
- Substitutes: Amazon may show your ad to shoppers who view the detail pages of products similar to yours.
- Complements: Amazon may show your ad to shoppers who view the detail pages of products that complement your product.

I could be wrong but I doubt there will be many occasions where complements or substitutes would work very well for books. Either way, you can bid separately for each match type so they are worth trying out and reviewing from time to time. They can all be altered once your campaign is running so you could just leave them all at your default bid at this stage.

Manual Targeting

If you clicked on manual targeting at the top of the page, then you will see another window show up here. This gives us two target types, keyword targeting or product targeting.

You'll also see another two more windows below this where you can enter keywords, products and negative targeting. I won't show them here, we'll go over these in the next few chapters.

Ad Copy

If you chose "Custom text ad" in the earlier option, here is where you will enter your Ad copy. You won't see this window if you opted for "Standard ad". Simply enter your ad copy in the text box, up to 150 characters. The ad preview below it will show what your ad will look like. To be honest, it doesn't show us much because it only shows one ad size (at the time of writing this). According to Amazon, this ad will only show at the bottom of the search page. I've never found this to be true. These ads can show up at the top, middle or bottom of the search pages and also as banner ads on detail pages, which is what the display ads used to do before they were discontinued. They do change things about often though so by the time you read this, things could be different.

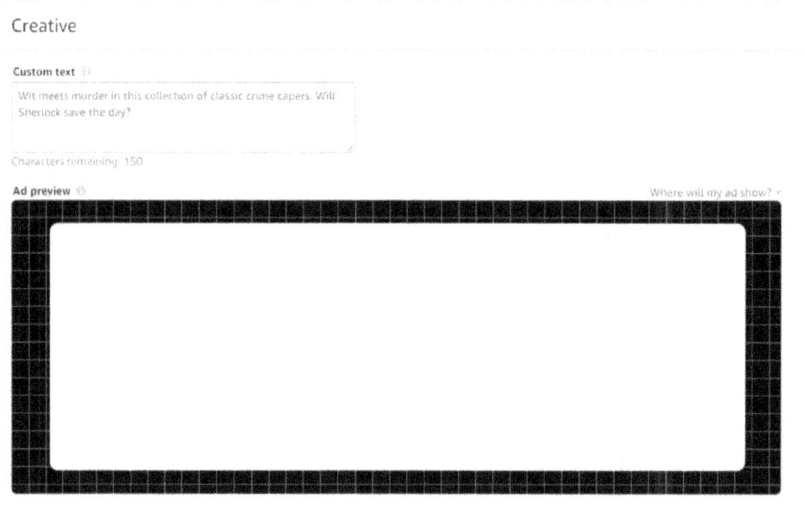

Where do the Ads show?

Sponsored ads show in various places on Amazon. If you use keyword targeting, your ads will show up on the search results pages if someone types in one of your ad's keywords (assuming you win the bid). Here are the first two books at the top of the search page for "how to start a business". They are both sponsored ads.

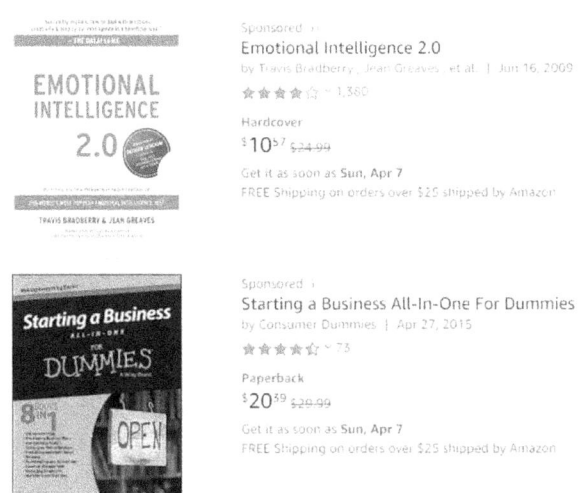

Neither of these ads are using ad copy so they have used the standard ad.

Here is a sponsored ad, with ad copy, (custom ad text) about halfway down the same search page.

Ad copy shown here

Your ad can also show up on the detail pages of other books. Here are two ad types in the sponsored carousel. One has ad copy and one doesn't.

Sponsored products related to this item

Ad copy

No Ad copy

Sponsored ads will sometimes show up as banner ads on detail pages, the same way that display ads used to before they were discontinued. At the moment these seem to show at random times so it's hard to know if Amazon are just experimenting with them at the moment.

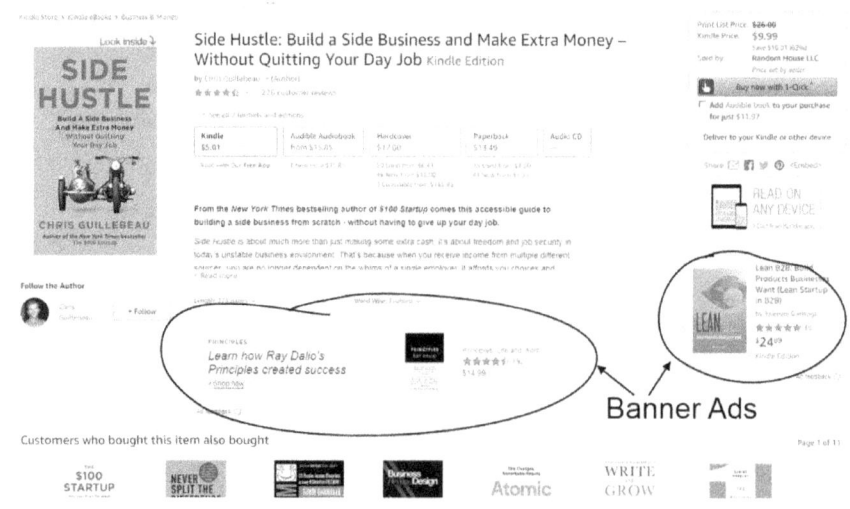

Banner Ads

Keyword Targeting

Sponsored product ads with manual targeting can apply to keywords, categories or specific products. Here we'll take a look at keyword targeting. This is where we bid on keywords that buyers might type into the search bar on Amazon or might relate to other books and authors you are trying to target. If our keyword gets triggered then our sponsored ad will show up in the search results or on a related book's detail page.

Assuming you have clicked on manual targeting and keyword targeting as described in the previous section, you'll get a window pop up that looks like this.

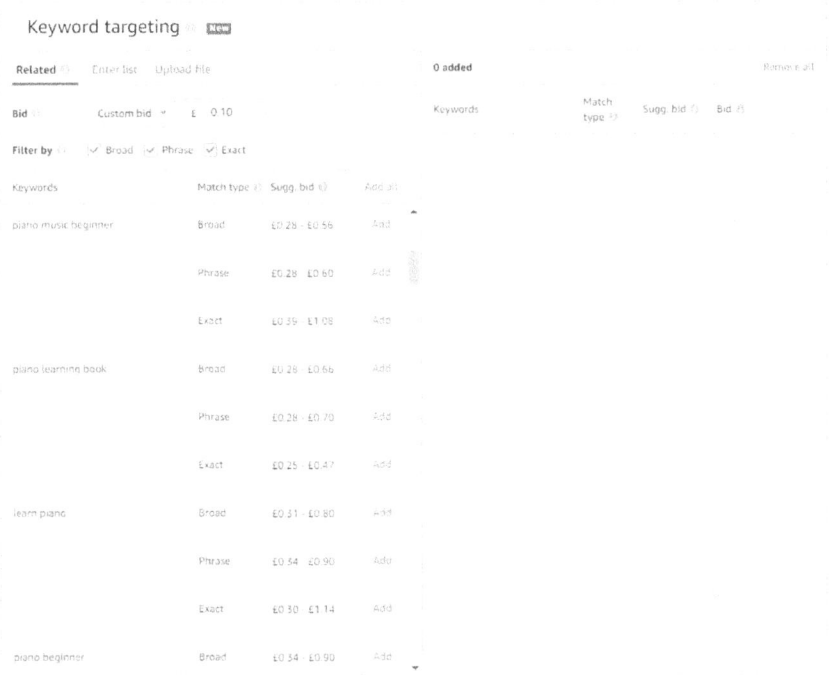

The first tab at the top will show a list of related keywords that Amazon think will be good for your book. If this list is empty then check that you have selected the book you want to advertise in the

"Products" window. Whether or not these keywords are a good choice, you will have to decide for yourself, just make sure that they look relevant to your book if you choose any of them which you do by clicking on the "Add" button to the right of each match type, which I'll explain in a moment. The keywords you add will get listed into the column on the right. You can also hide or show the three different match types by clicking the check boxes where it says filter.

Watch out for the bid amount. If you click on the bid button you can choose a custom bid, default bid or suggested bid. Unless you know exactly what you want to bid for each keyword then it's best to play safe here and start with a custom bid of around 0.10c to 0.20c.

If most of the suggested keywords look good to you then it may be easier to click the "Add all" button at the top and then remove the ones you don't want from right hand column by clicking the X at the right of each keyword, which will look like this.

Keyword targeting NEW

Keywords	Match type	Sugg. bid	Add all
piano music beginner	Broad	£0.28 - £0.56	Added
	Phrase	£0.26 - £0.65	Added
	Exact	£0.32 - £1.06	Added
piano learning book	Broad	£0.25 - £0.66	Added
	Phrase	£0.29 - £0.70	Added
	Exact	£0.25 - £0.47	Added
learn piano	Broad	£0.31 - £0.80	Added
	Phrase	£0.34 - £0.90	Added
	Exact	£0.50 - £1.14	Added
piano beginner	Broad	£0.34 - £0.90	Added

198 added Remove all

Keywords	Match type	Sugg. bid	Bid	
piano beginner book	Broad	£0.44 (£0.37 - £0.92)	£ 0.10	X
piano beginner book	Phrase	£0.58 (£0.31 - £0.76)	£ 0.10	X
piano beginner book	Exact	£0.75 (£0.29 - £0.4)	£ 0.10	X
adult learn piano book	Broad		£ 0.10	X
adult learn piano book	Phrase		£ 0.10	X
adult learn piano book	Exact		£ 0.10	X
piano music beginner	Phrase	£0.59 (£0.28 - £0.6)	£ 0.10	X
piano music beginner	Exact	£0.54 (£0.5 - £1.06)	£ 0.10	X
piano learning book	Phrase	£0.3 (£0.28 - £0.70)	£ 0.10	X
piano learning book	Exact	£0.35 (£0.25 - £0.47)	£ 0.10	X
learn piano	Phrase	£0.45 (£0.34 - £0.90)	£ 0.10	X

Match types

The match type you choose will affect how your keyword will get triggered when somebody searches for it.

Broad: This will get the most clicks and give you the least control. Let's say you have the keyword "play piano". A broad match will pretty much leave it up to Amazon to decide. It will use the words in any order, include plurals and other words that Amazon may think are related. Any of the search terms below could trigger your keyword.

Learn to play piano
How to play piano
How to play the piano
How to play piano songs
Lessons for piano to play songs
Play and learn piano for beginners

Phrase: With phrase match, your keyword will only get triggered by the same sequence of words. For instance, if you have the keyword "how to play piano" as a phrase match then that exact phrase will need to be typed into search, in the correct order but can include other words. For example, these search terms can trigger your ad:

How to play piano for beginners
How to play piano chords
Learn how to play piano
Exercises for learning how to play piano

Exact: This match type does what it says. It will only show your ad if the person searches for your keyword exactly as written. If you bid for exact match "how to play piano" then that will need to be typed into search, exactly in that order, with no additional words.

Enter List

Clicking on the "Enter list" tab will open a different area where you can enter your own keywords manually. You do so by typing (or copy and pasting) keywords and phrases into the window below. It's worth typing out a few ideas as a window of suggestions will pop up as you type which might give you some good ideas. Once you are done, click on the Add keywords button and your keywords will be added to the right hand column, one for each match type you have the check boxes ticked.

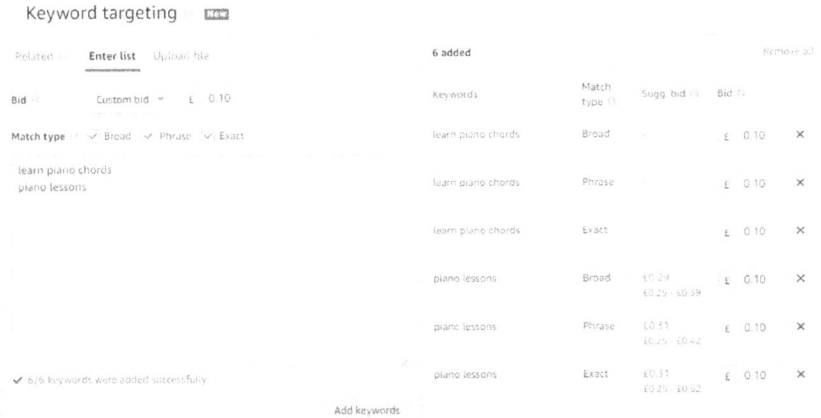

Upload file

The last tab in this window allows you to upload a spreadsheet with your keywords, match type and bid. This is only worth it if you have a very large list of keywords with many bid variations and match types. If you want to do this, the best way is to download the template which you can edit in something like Excel or Google Sheets.

Click here to
download template

Product Targeting Categories

Product targeting allows you to manually choose where to show your ads, either on individual book detail pages, or other books belonging to various categories. Let's start with categories.

Assuming you have clicked on manual targeting and product targeting as described earlier, you'll get a window pop up that looks like this.

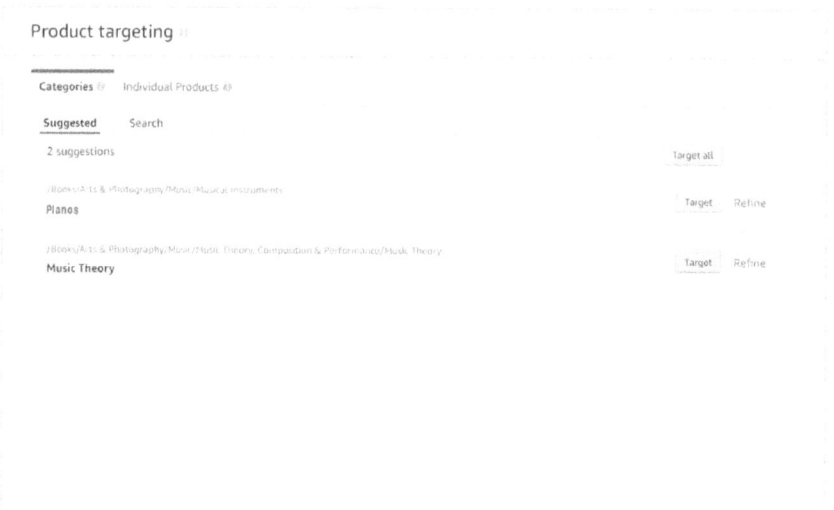

The first tab shows suggested categories that Amazon thinks will be good for your book. If you like what you see then click on the Target button to add the category to your list. In this window you will also notice a refine option where you can choose only to show up on books or brands within a certain price range or review rating. I've never tried this, it may have its uses, unfortunately there seems to be no way to alter it afterwards. Unless you already have data on your books showing that most of your sales come from detail pages of books within particular ranges, then I'd say don't bother with it.

The suggested categories will only be what Amazon think will suit your book. I have had good results by adding other categories to the list, as long as they are relevant. You can choose more categories by clicking on the search tab (see image below). You can drill down for categories or use the search bar to find potential categories worth adding.

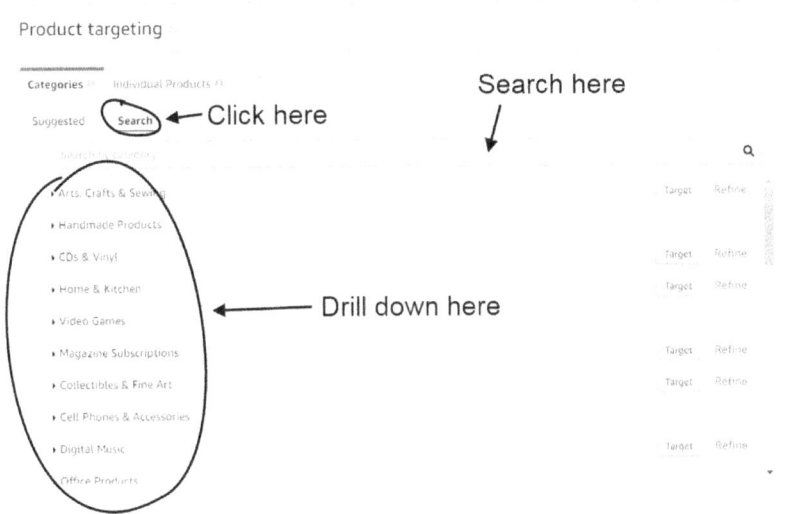

Where do these ads show up?

Category ads, as far as I can tell, only show up in the sponsored products carousel on detail pages of books listed in those categories. So far, I've not found any evidence that they show anywhere else. Category ads are quite new (early 2019) and can burn your money quite quickly. This doesn't mean they are bad, so far they are proving to work very well for many people, but be careful and don't be tempted to just add hundreds of general categories and hope for the best. While this strategy might quickly show you what works and what doesn't, be very careful with your budget and bid prices and don't forget to keep a regular eye on them. Also bear in mind that adding lots of categories is likely to harm your relevancy.

Targeting Individual Products

The last ad type we have is to target individual products, i.e., specific books. The options are very similar to adding categories, only this time we target specific books. Three tabs are available; Suggested, Search, Enter list. The suggested tab may or may not show some suggestions for you. In the search tab you can either enter a book title, ASIN or try a general phrase to try to find similar books. In the screenshot below you will see a list of products that show up when I enter the term "learn piano".

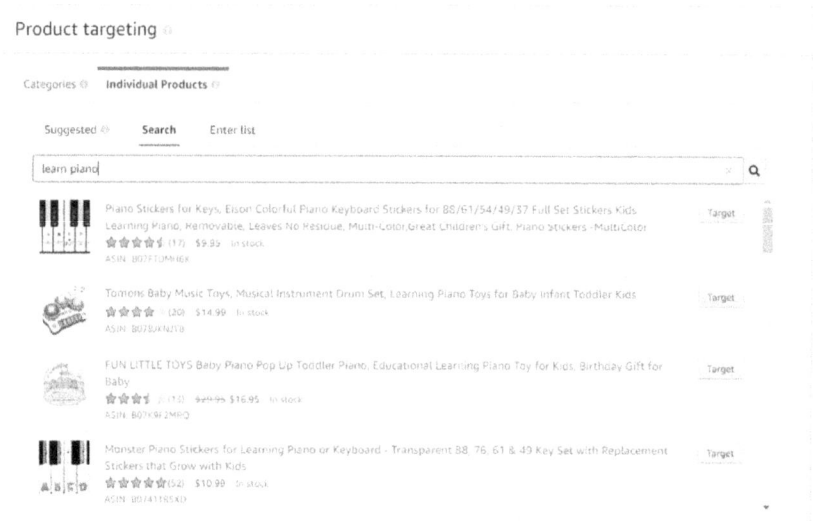

Be careful not to blindly click and target anything that shows up here, as you can see in the image above, I get a list of products that are not necessarily books. You can try searching for something like "learn piano book" or other search phrases that you can scroll through and look for books that you feel are worth targeting.

The chances are that you will have a few very specific books that you want to target or you might have a large list of ASINs that you have collected or pulled from search reports, in which case you can copy them straight out of a spreadsheet or text file and paste them into the "Enter list" window, shown below.

You can get a book's ASIN by going to its detail page on Amazon and scroll down to where the product details are.

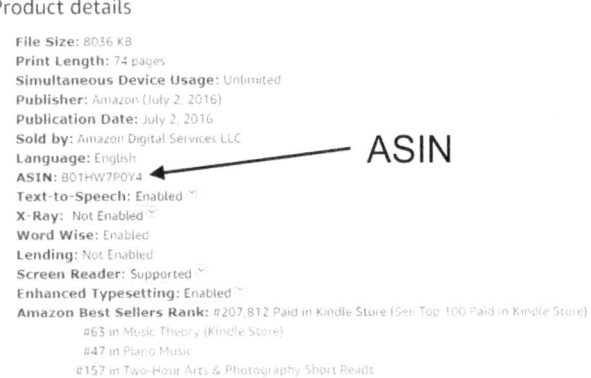

The paperback and Kindle version of the same book will be different so bear that in mind if you want to target both. The paperback will have ISBN numbers, you can enter the ISBN-10 number in your list. If you don't already have a list of ASINs ready to go then this will obviously take time to build a large list. You can however add more ASINs anytime after your campaign is running.

Negative Keywords

The last set of options we can include with our manual targeting campaigns are negative keywords or products. This is where we can add search terms, or ASINs that that we *don't* want our ads to show up for. Depending on whether you have chosen product targeting or keyword targeting, you'll get an appropriate window where you can add ASINs or keywords.

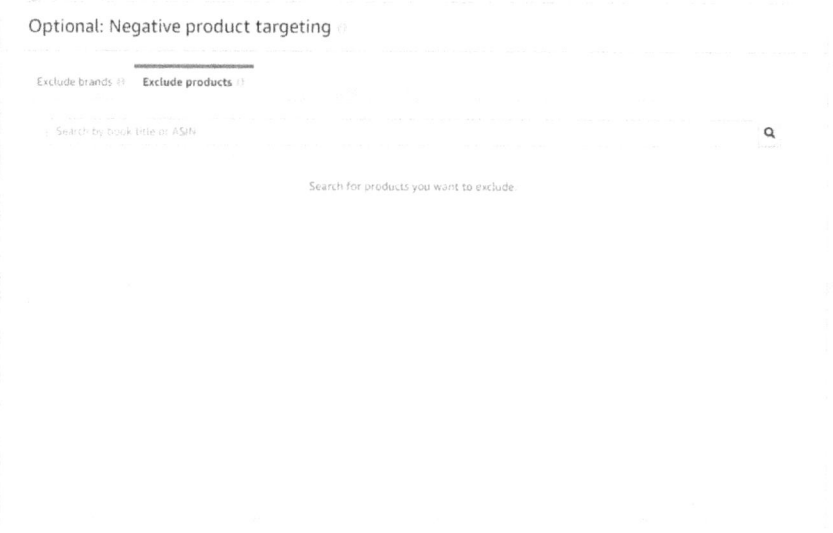

Negative product targeting is straightforward. Simply enter the ASINs of the detail pages that you do not want your book to show up on. You are only likely to use this for category targeting or if you want to temporarily disable a targeted product without actually removing it from your product list, although I've never tested this to see if one overrides the other in this case. If however you are using category targeting then this can be useful as categories will show a very broad range of books. Either way, you probably won't bother to use this until you have run an ad campaign for long enough to gather some data.

Negative keyword targeting *(optional)*

Match type ☑ Negative exact ☑ Negative phrase

Enter your list and separate each item with a new line.

0 added

Keywords

Remove all

Match type

With negative keyword targeting, however, you might have more logical reasons to add a few negative keywords at the beginning. Personally, in most cases I would still let an ad run without any negative targeting until it has gathered some data.

Negative keywords can be exact or phrase. Exact is self explanatory, if we add an exact phrase "learn how to play blues piano" then your ad will not show when somebody types in that exact phrase, as written. On the other hand, "how to play blues piano for beginners" would not be blocked.

With phrase match we could negative target "for beginners". In this case "how to play blues piano for beginners" will not show our ad because it contains our negative phrase. If your book is aimed at advanced pianists then you could add a negative phrase "beginners". This will then prevent your ad showing for any search term that includes the word "beginners".

Adding negative keywords is done much the same as adding keywords. Just type the phrase you want and then click the add keywords button. Be sure first to select the appropriate check box for whether you want exact or phrase. If both are checked then you'll get both types added to the right hand column.

Again, most of the time, unless we're quite sure right from the start, negative keywords are best added after the ad campaign has been running for long enough to collect data that we can use to find keywords which are getting us clicks but no sales. Thanks to the recently introduced search term reports, we now have access to this data in our KDP advertising reports. More on this a bit later when we get into optimisation.

Bidding Strategy - Dynamic Bids

Campaign bidding strategy is a fairly recent (and confusing)
change to Amazon Advertising and has replaced what used to be
called Bid+. Before we get into the explanation, let's take a look at
how you can access it. The first option is to to set it up when you
initially create a new campaign and it looks like this (from the
create new campaign page):

If you click at the bottom of the window where it says "Adjust
bids by placement (replaces Bid+)" it will open a further option for
placement, which then looks like this.

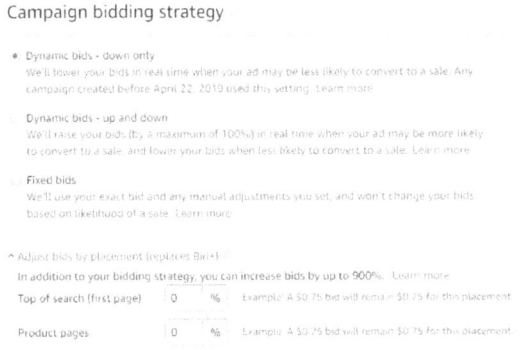

Although you can make changes here, this is not really the best
time to set up dynamic bidding so it's best left at default which is

"Dynamic bids - down only," which should be selected and both placement types left at 0%. The reason for this is because dynamic bidding works best when your ad has been running for some time and gathered some data, giving the algorithms some time to work out what might be good or bad for your book. Personally I would let the ad run for a few weeks first before experimenting with any of this unless you already know what you are doing.

Bidding strategy and placement can be set and changed at any time from within the campaign itself once it's running. To access it just click on your campaign from the dashboard and then click "Campaign settings" in the left column.

Scroll down the campaign settings page and you will see where you can set dynamic bids and placements which looks like this.

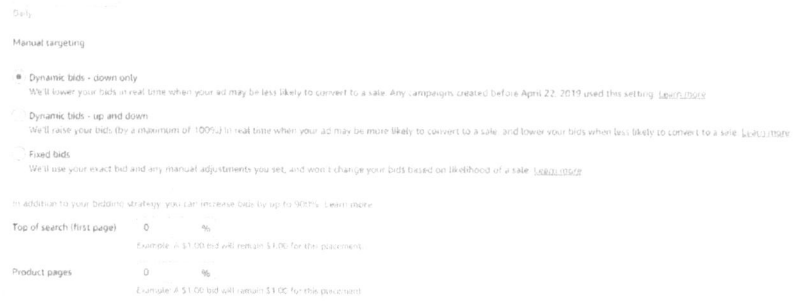

Placements can also be accessed from clicking on "Placements" in the left hand menu of the campaign. They are not separate, just different areas to access the same thing. If you make changes here, it will be reflected in the campaign settings page and vice-versa.

That's the easy bit. Now the fun part - trying to make sense of it all! Be very careful here and make sure you have it fully understood before going too crazy. This is where you can turn a $1 bid into a $20 bid if you aren't paying attention.

Bids, dynamic bids and placements are three separate things but all work together, per campaign. Think of dynamic bids and placements as multipliers to your actual bid. You can visualise it something like this.

$$\boxed{\text{Bid Amount}} + \boxed{\text{Dynamic Bid}} + \boxed{\text{Placement \%}} = \boxed{\text{Total Bid}}$$

Bid Amount

This will be the cost of your actual bid per keyword, product or category, whichever one gets triggered in the campaign. For an auto keyword campaign it will be the bid you have set for the targeting group that gets triggered. If you've not made any changes here then it should be the same as your default bid. You can view your targeting groups by clicking on "Targeting" in the left hand menu of an auto keyword campaign. The image below shows one of my auto campaigns with a default bid of 0.25c but as you can see, I'm actually bidding 0.40c for Loose match. Just remember to check if you aren't sure.

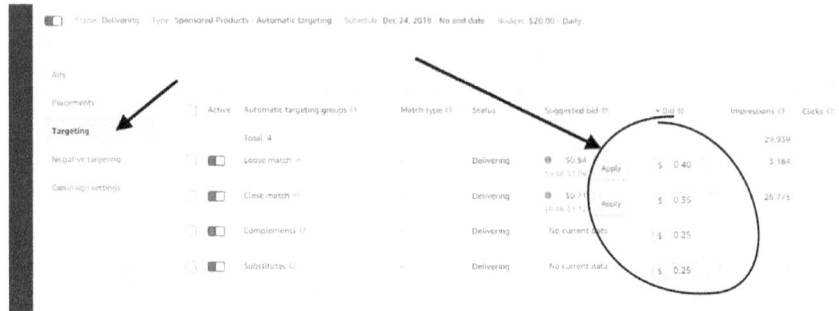

Essentially, the bid amount is going to be the cost of whatever gets triggered in the campaign. Dynamic bidding and placements affect the entire campaign so always look at your highest bid, whether that's a keyword, ASIN, category or targeting group and use that as your possible maximum bid amount.

Dynamic Bids

Dynamic bidding is where we put our trust in the Amazon algorithms to decide when it might be worth us bidding higher or lower than normal based on the likelihood of us getting a sale. We have no idea how this is actually decided so let's just take a hypothetical situation which we can wrap our head around without too much difficulty. It might also help realise the importance of relevancy and why too many keywords and variations in a single campaign isn't always a good idea.

Imagine you are selling a book called "How to build a shed". There are ten advertisers bidding for the search term "how to build a shed". There are only two sponsored ad spots at the top of the search page and coincidentally all ten bidders are bidding the exact same amount. Whose ads will Amazon show? There's almost certainly some sort of scoring system going on which is probably (I'm guessing) decided by multiple factors including: how many times a book has made a sale from that keyword; how well does the keyword match the book's title; the bid amount.

There are probably other things taken into consideration like reviews, refund rates, KU page read, probably even the buying history of the person actually searching etc. We don't know, we can only guess. Either way, with this kind of information available, Amazon can decide what book and its associated ad is more worthy of the top spot. I have seen plenty of evidence to prove that the highest bid alone does not always trump other factors. All of these things will affect the actual worth of everything you bid for. If we put our trust in Amazon getting this right ... that's where dynamic bids come into play and we get three options.

1: Down only
However it decides, if Amazon thinks a click on your ad will be less likely to make a sale then it may decrease your bid. Your click cost will never exceed your bid amount but can be lower.

2: Up and down
Your bid can be decreased just like down only but also can be increased up to 100% for the top of the search results page and up to 50% for everywhere else.

3: Fixed bids
A fixed bid is exactly what it says. You will always pay your bid amount for every click. This might sound like a crazy idea but really it's down to how well the algorithms are doing in determining your ad's "worth". If you think Amazon is getting it all wrong then fixed bids might just be worth a try. For example, down only bidding might be lowering your bids for some

keywords that would be better left unaltered. The only way to find this out is to try it and see.

Placements

Amazon use three placement terms to describe areas of the Amazon website. Top of search, product pages and rest of search.

Top of search refers to the one or two ads that you might see at the top of the first search results page. Rest of search includes sponsored ads in the middle or bottom of the first page and all sponsored ads from the second page and beyond. Product pages refers to ads shown on product detail pages such as the sponsored ads carousels and (currently) banner ads or those shown on shopping cart and checkout pages.

We can increase the bids up to 900% for top of search or product pages. We can't make placement bid increases for the rest of search.

In Practice

With dynamic bidding we don't have any control over where the ad gets shown or triggered. If we use dynamic up and down and the ad happens to get triggered at the top of search then we could be looking at a 100% increase over our normal bid amount. This then gets passed on to our placement bid increases which are then further increased to a maximum of our specified percentage.

For example, if we are bidding 0.50c for a keyword using dynamic bidding - up and down, we could end up paying $1 for the click if it's shown at the top of search (max 100% increase). If the placement bid is also set at 100% for top of search then a further 100% increase will raise this to a potential $2 bid.

If the same keyword gets triggered on a product page then dynamic bidding could raise this by a maximum of 50% so our bid could be raised to 0.75c. If we have the placement bid for product pages at 100% then this would be doubled to $1.50.

If we felt that top of search was not our best place to show ads, and we normally get better results from product page ads, then we could use dynamic bidding down only with product page placements set at a percentage we are prepared to pay. Let's say that is 50% and we are bidding 0.50c. In effect, what we are telling Amazon is that we are prepared to pay up to 0.75c to get shown on product pages but for all other bids leave it at 0.50c.

Just remember the formula: bid amount + dynamic bid type + placement increase = total potential bid. Therefore a bid of $1 with dynamic bidding up and down - and a placement or 900% could turn your $1 bid into a possible $20 bid. This doesn't necessarily mean you will pay the full $20 but it would mean you are prepared to pay up to $20 for a single click.

Is it worth it?

That's the big question. I haven't experimented enough with dynamic and placement bidding to really be certain. When I have used it, sales have certainly increased but also so have my costs. I don't have enough data to determine if this "likelihood of sale" dynamic would increase my sales any different from just leaving everything at default and simply increasing my normal bid amount.

I think it should be experimented with but you need to work smart and keep a close eye on it. There are a few things to think about. First let's say that we have a manual keyword campaign with hundreds of keywords and we turn on dynamic bidding (up and down) and also add 100% placement increases. We run the campaign for two weeks and find that our ACoS has increased. We could easily assume it isn't worth it and set it all back to default. In actual fact, we wouldn't really have any idea whether it worked or not - it may be that it worked great, we just can't see how.

The problem here is that the settings are global for the campaign. It may be that for one of our keywords the dynamic bid increase worked brilliantly and increased sales leading to a lowered ACoS. Unfortunately the rest of our keywords all performed badly which offset the overall campaign ACoS. It may even be that for some of the keywords, extra sales came from the placement increase and not the dynamic bid increase. Unfortunately the placement reports are very much lacking in any detail. This makes it very difficult to analyse what's really going on.

For Auto keyword and category campaigns we have even less control and analytical potential. All we could do is set; wait; hope for the best. This isn't to say it's not worth trying, it just means that if we try it out and it doesn't work - it doesn't necessarily conclude that dynamic bidding doesn't work.

When we make changes to anything it's vital that we don't make too many changes at any one time. In the example above using a manual keyword campaign with hundreds of keywords and then setting dynamic up and down, with both placement increases set to 100%, with all changes made at the same time - is not a good way to experiment with something unless we have access to very detailed reports, which unfortunately we don't. If you want to try out dynamic bidding then it's probably best to work with small campaigns that you can manage and analyse easier. This will be best done with fairly small manual keyword or product targeting campaigns, this way we can test it out in a somewhat controlled environment.

Running and Optimising your Ads

Once your ad campaigns are running, you will need to monitor and refine them. There is no sense in trying to decipher anything from them until you have collected a decent amount of data. This could be days, but more likely weeks, possibly longer. We are mostly looking for two things. Campaigns that are wasting money and campaigns that are not spending enough. I use the term campaign in its broader sense: this could mean keywords, categories or targeted products.

If you read the advice in many forums and discussion groups, people will often recommend using high daily budgets for each campaign in the belief that the algorithms will give it more weight. Personally, I'm not convinced but I have no proof of this so I could be wrong. Either way, it's a bad way to start out if you've never run Amazon ads before. You should start by getting a feel for it and covering yourself just in case you mess up and Amazon takes a whole load of your money. Budgets can be changed at any time so don't go mad with them at first.

The other piece of advice you will get is to run many campaigns, possibly hundreds, and use thousands of keywords. Again, I think this is a bad idea. Until you are very familiar with all of this, the worse thing you can do is make things more confusing than they need to be. Running hundreds of ads and thousands of keywords creates a minefield for you to sort through and get any kind of idea of what you are doing. Fine for advanced advertisers, not so clever for the inexperienced. Here's the thing about running a large amount of adverts: if you can't get just a handful of ad campaigns working, then stacking them up is going to work against you in many ways. Advanced users that have a large number of ad campaigns, do so by building data and refining over time. Doing it all in one go will mean it takes you far longer, and probably costs you more in the long run. It might even create long term damage to your book's selling ability because it will possibly weaken your book's relevance.

Let's say you have setup four separate campaigns for a single book: an auto, category, product and a keyword campaign. If you have these running for a week or so and you are not getting any clicks or sales, worst still hardly any impressions then repeating the process will not help you, something else is wrong and it will just create a mess in your advertising dashboard, making it harder to decipher anything.

The one thing you will learn from running Amazon ads is this: what you think you know ... you probably don't. For example, you might be convinced that you know what kind of reader will enjoy your book but the results can often surprise you. This is why we need to collect data before we make too many assumptions. You might feel certain that your book should be in a particular category and targeting books by specific authors that you believe are a perfect match, but in reality, sales can come from where you least expect them. Not definitely, but very possible. Less likely in non-fiction but even here things can surprise you occasionally.

Sometimes it's Amazon that have things wrong and not you. One example is the category Kindle eBooks .../ Music. The majority of this category's top 100 is filled with Rockstar Romance. The thing is, this category is under non-fiction. Take a look at the screenshot below.

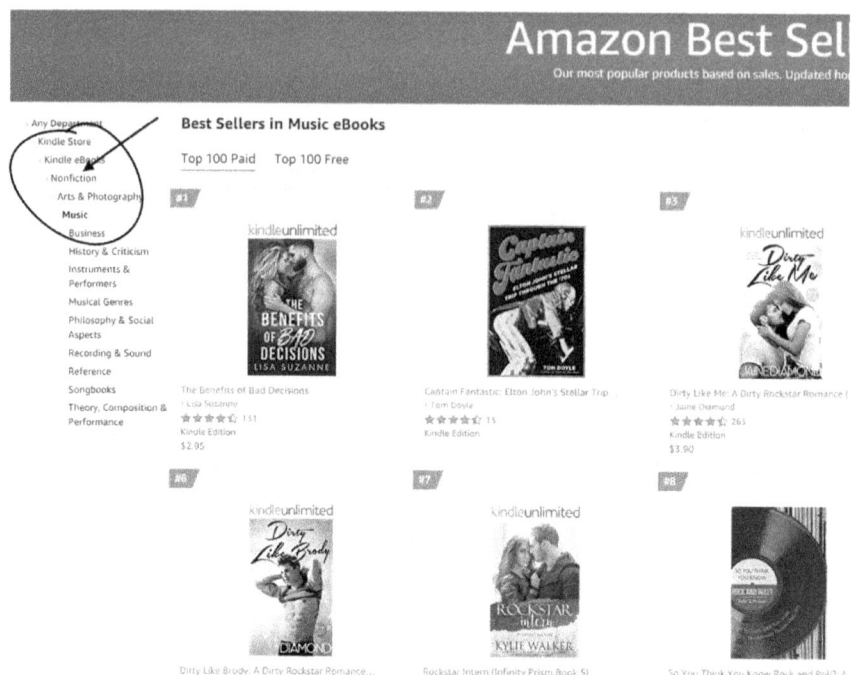

Now don't get me wrong, I don't know how Amazon likes to think about categorising books, but I do know this. If I were selling a romance novel, whether it's about Rockstars or not, I doubt I would have thought about advertising in the Arts & Photography category when creating a targeted category sponsored ad.

This is why we need to do our research when we pick categories for our books. Even though this seems like a wrong category, it's one of those instances where we could safely assume that this will not harm our relevance. If that category is filled with related books then the Amazon system must think it's the right category.

What you would not want to do in this case is try to drill down even further in the hope of getting less competition. For example, if we drill down the music category we will find many sub-categories. Most of these romance books seem to be about country or rock musicians and can be found in the *Musical Genres* sub-categories under Rock and Country. See image below.

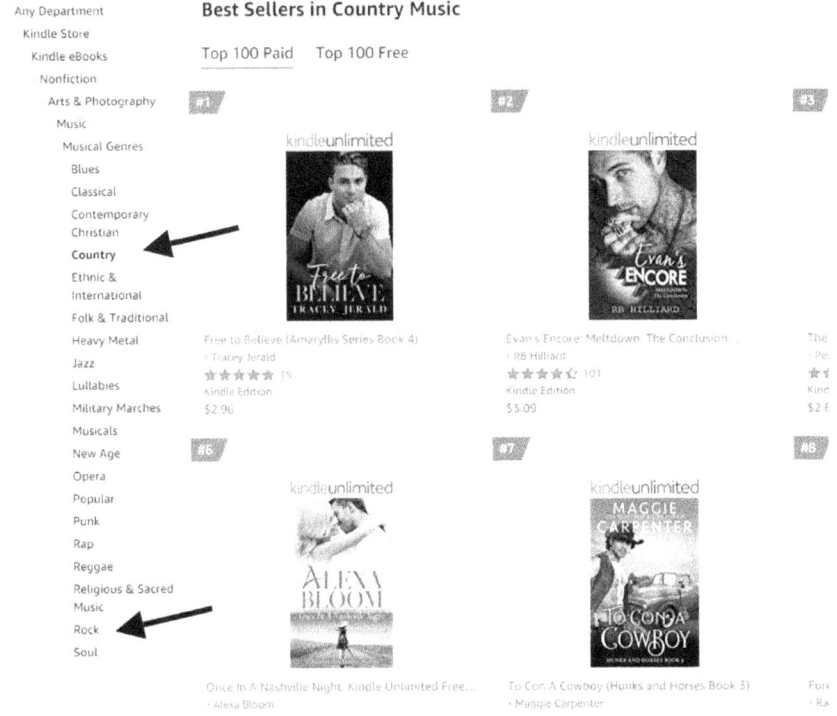

Where you might need to be careful is let's say your book is a romance novel about a blues musician, it would probably be wise to NOT list it in the blues category. Why? Because if you look in that category you will find it dominated by "learn blues guitar"

and similar music educational books. Does this mean your book wouldn't sell in this category? To be honest, I don't know, but I think it highly likely that Amazon will consider this a musical instrument / educational category. You might be more sensible to just list it either among the Rockstar / Country categories or don't drill down and just target Arts & Photography / Music. None of this is guaranteed but the more you try to stay relevant, the more chance you will have of success. Of course if all else fails then you could certainly try experimenting with these things, just be warned that you might be confusing the algorithms further and show up in front of the wrong audience.

The main thing with category targeting is you should research books that you think are closely related to your book. Find as many as you can and look for the common categories that the majority of them belong to. These are most likely the categories you should target and maybe bid a little higher. Again, be careful of bad advice. Many authors will target as many categories as possible in the hope of gaining some traction and getting more impressions. This does make some sense but still avoid straying too far away from what your book is about. You might find you get a few extra sales but in the process you might also be screwing up your relevancy and your "also-boughts". For example, if you have a romance novel and try to advertise it in a thriller category, you might just happen to get some sales. If those sales exceed the sales you get from romance related categories, the Amazon algorithms might think your book is more likely to be a thriller, which in turn means it will try selling to the wrong audience. This can result in the eventual ceasing up of sales because the more Amazon shows your book to who it believes are the correct audience, that audience doesn't respond very well, your book could get "marked" as a poor seller, so Amazon will just start showing it less often and you will have to start bidding higher to try overcome it.

The same thing goes if you are targeting specific products. Don't just hit and hope. Make sure the books you target are likely to attract the right audience. You might be somebody who reads many different genres, don't assume everybody else does. Sure, there might be thousands of people that will read thrillers as well as romance. Thousands, however, are not enough. Majority is what you are going after. I don't read fiction personally so I can't say what is typical, but for the many years I have been in business, people generally behave similarly in groups. I'll use non-fiction as an example here.

Musical instrument learning is a big market. There are a lot of musicians who play multiple instruments. With this in mind, it would make some sense in targeting guitarists with a piano teaching book, so I could advertise my book in the piano category, as well as guitar and harmonica etc. Chances are I will get some sales. The problem is that with each sale I make to the wrong audience, I'm not making it easy for Amazon algorithms to figure out who best to target my book to. Let's work with some hypothetical numbers to illustrate my point. Out of 10,000 musicians, 5000 are pianists, 2000 are guitarists and 500 play harmonica. So I could run an ad campaign and select three categories: piano, guitar and harmonica. I also find the top selling books in the same three categories and target those as well. Bear with me here ...

I set a bid of 0.50c across the board. If the competitiveness of each category is in the same order from high to low, what might happen is my ad will show up higher on the search page for harmonica. I may also show on the first page scroll of the sponsored carousel. For guitar I show up somewhere in the middle and for piano I might show somewhere near the end. Being first in the list makes a big difference. There's a good chance

I will sell more piano books to harmonica players, simply because some of them play both instruments and I'm getting seen at the top. If I start to sell more books in the harmonica category then Amazon will possibly think my book is about harmonica. This doesn't necessarily mean all my piano category ads and keywords will stop working, but it might result in those ads being pushed down and force me to start bidding higher because Amazon now thinks my book is not relevant to piano, it's about harmonica.

If on the other hand I made sure my targeting was relevant, then with each sale I'm adding weight to my ad's position in that category, therefore I can move further up the page and possibly even reduce my bid over time. The bottom line here is this, if we put more emphasis on the "majority" then people looking for piano books are only looking for piano books. Trying to grab one or two outliers here and there is not always a good strategy.

Now with that said, these are things you should just be considering. I'm not saying only be 100% relevant at all costs, but definitely try to keep within in a fairly tight area of relevance. Amazon algorithms aren't completely stupid but they aren't magic and they aren't human. Your book title, KDP category selection, keywords in the book description will all go a long way towards making your book more relevant, as long as there is enough info to go on. Just be mindful that every click and every non-relevant sale can sway your relevancy over time and ultimately bring your sales to a stop. If you just happen to get lucky and make a lot of regular sales then all of the above becomes slightly less important. However, if you are struggling to make many sales then all of this becomes very important.

Auto targeting ads can remove a lot of these problems for us because there's not really much we can do with them other than set the bid price. Auto ads can be a bit hit and miss but since the introduction of search reports, it now makes a lot of sense to keep an auto ad running because we can get a lot of good information out of the search reports. More on this a bit later.

Auto targeting is left in the hands of the algorithms. We can assume that they are self learning, this is why we need to leave them running. If your book is new and had no sales then the learning algorithms don't have a lot to go on, other than the book title, subtitle and keywords in the 7 keyword fields, keywords used in the description and the selected categories. If your book is fiction then the title and book description might not help much unless they include related keywords, not always easy with fiction. This is why we need to leave the ads running. It's probable that the algorithms try showing the ad in places that it think might be relevant and then auto-refine as it learns. Hopefully the ad will get a few sales and when it does, it starts to figure out the type of reader it should target. The more sales you get from an auto ad, the better it should perform over time, but even if it doesn't, as long as you are getting impressions and clicks, you will be able to figure out from the reports what isn't working.

Keyword targeted ads can also work very well, but like auto-ads, they need to be refined over time, only difference is that you do this manually. Non-fiction should be a lot easier to find good keywords for but also can be quite expensive. Don't let this put you off. If you cannot afford to chance too much of your budget then just bid low. Over time you will still get some data to work with and find out what kinds of keywords work, or don't work.

Dashboard Updates

Since I start writing this book, Amazon have changed the look of the dashboard. Most of the screenshots in the following chapters were taken before the changes. I can no longer recapture the same date ranges used so most of what you see from here on out will be images of the old dashboard.

The good news is it's only the layout that has changed so everything here still applies. Some things have moved in position, for instance, things like the "Create campaign" and "Date range" button has moved from above to below the graph. Most of the tabs for reports, campaign targeting etc., have been moved to the left of the screen as shown below.

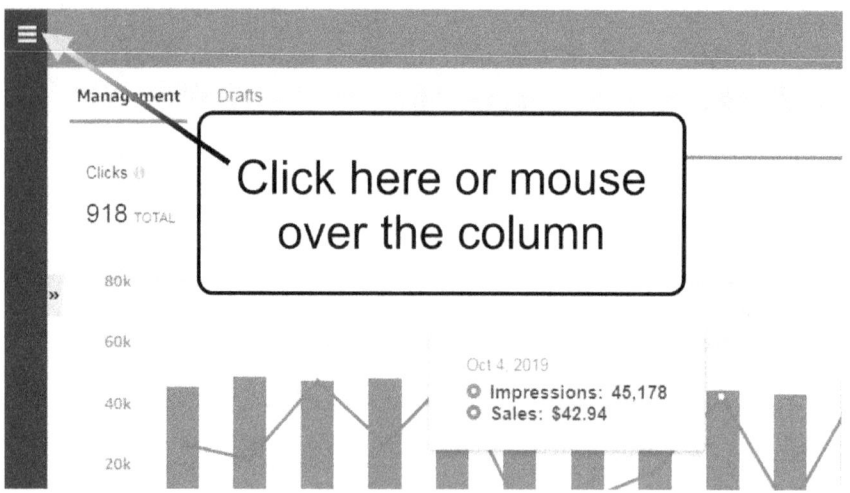

Clicking on the hamburger icon or moving your mouse over to the left column as shown above will open up the left of the screen where you can get to the report tabs etc., which should look like this:

The other tabs that were previously accessed above the timeline graphs from within the campaigns have also been moved to the left column and looks like this...

These are the only major differences (so far) and no functionality has been changed so just be aware that many of the images in the following sections will look slightly different to the current dashboard layout.

The Dashboard

The Amazon advertising dashboard is where we monitor what's going on with our ads. If you have only just started running ads then you won't be getting much useful information so you will need to wait for data to build up. In the following pages we shall take a look at how we can interpret the charts and see how our ads are performing. Before we do that, let's take a little tour around the dashboard. This is what you will see when you login to your Amazon advertising account.

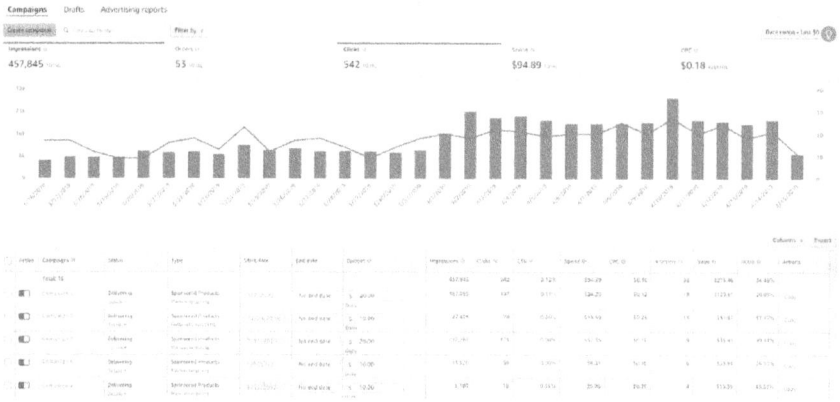

Unfortunately, like everything modern and web based, it's been designed by idiots and so will be much easier to use if you have a wide screen. It will still work on smaller screens but you will have to deal with annoying scroll bars.

Columns

You can however hide some of the columns that you don't need to look at so often. They can be changed easily at any time by clicking on the columns button just above the far right column.

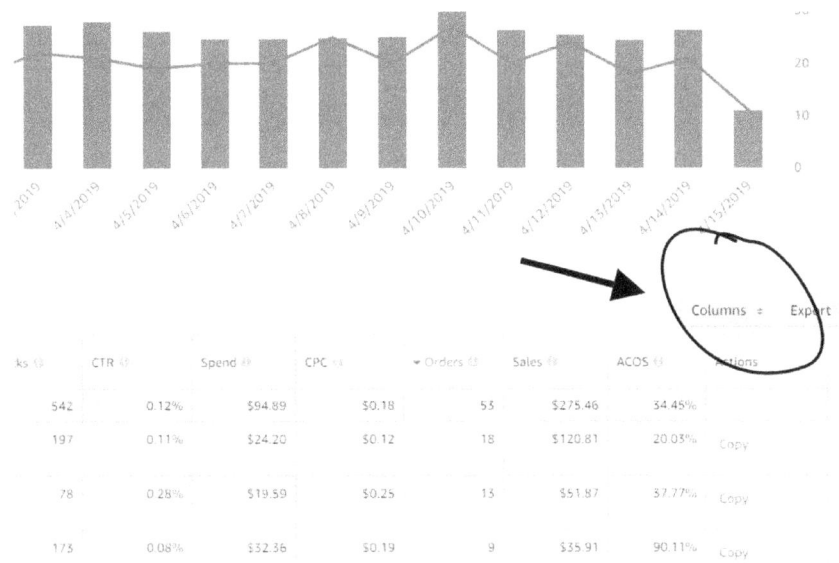

Click this button and then click again on "Customize columns" to bring up the column picker. Here you can choose which columns to display.

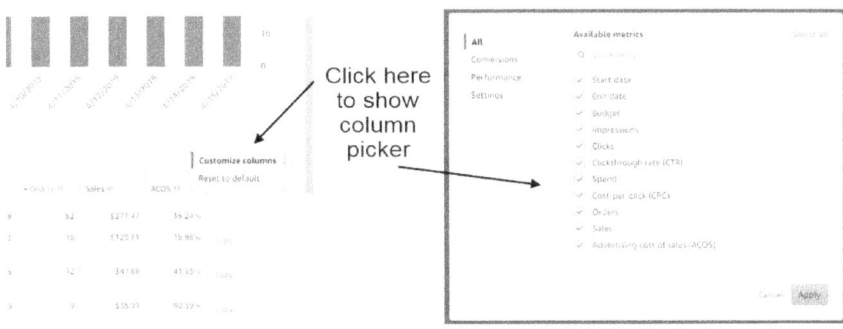

I rarely look at budget or date settings so I might decide to hide those if I need more screen space.

Date

You can adjust the date range in your dashboard for any range up to 90 days with daily increments or for the year-to-date and lifetime with monthly increments. This is very useful for trying to see changes over time periods, you will probably use this quite a lot to look out for changes that you make, which you should keep a separate note of. For instance, you might increase the bids on a campaign at the beginning of March, you can then use the timeline view to see if you had a boost in sales etc.

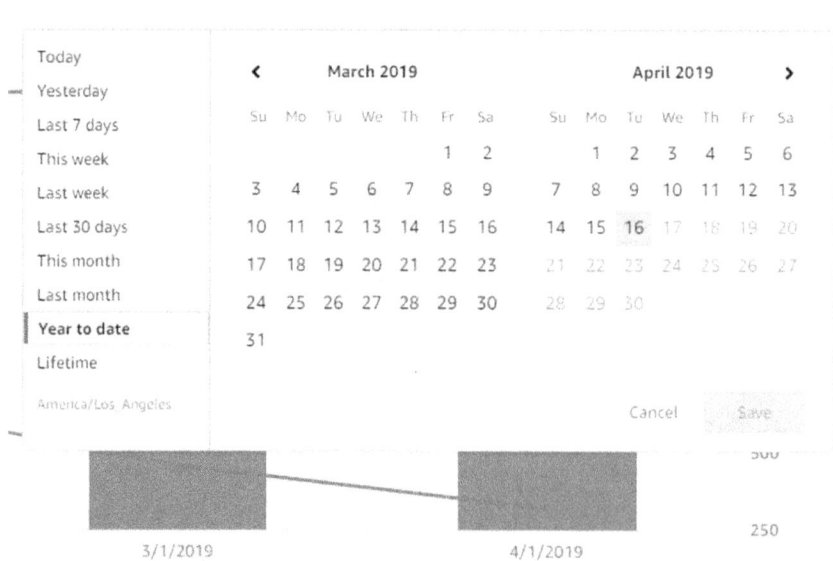

Metrics

The timeline graph allows you to see any two metrics at one time.
You can choose these by clicking on the metric buttons above the
graph which will toggle them on and off.

You can view more metrics by closing one of them. Do this by
clicking on the "x" of the one you want to switch and then click the
"Add metric" button.

Filter

The filter is used to narrow down and look at single campaigns or
search by a number of factors like impressions, clicks etc. You can

further narrow down with operators to search for numbers "greater than" or "equals" and so on. This is an incredibly handy function for filtering out things we don't want included in our charts, unfortunately it's a bit flaky and doesn't always work properly. The new dashboard is still only a few months old so hopefully this will get fixed in the not too distant future. Let's take a look at a few examples of using the filter.

If you are on the main page you can type one of your campaign names into the search field and click the filter button or hit the Enter key. This will update the graph and the column data to only show data for that campaign.

If for some reason you only want to see something like all campaigns with 20 or more clicks, you can use the filter. First make sure the search field is empty and then click on the "Filter by" button which will bring up a list of the things you can search for. For this example we will choose "Clicks".

You will then see a set of options where you can choose your criteria. We will choose "greater than or equal to" and type 20 into the field: then click the Save button.

All of the other filter options work the same way so it's just a matter of choosing what you want and use the options you have available.

Campaigns

You can click on any of the campaigns in the first column to show the data and settings for each campaign individually. Everything will be similar to above but with additional tabs for selecting and viewing keywords, categories or products depending on the type of campaign you originally setup. All of the available options are separated by tabs (which are now in the sidebar as discussed in the previous chapter).

We are mostly interested in the "Targeting" tab as that's where we will spend most of our time. All other tabs should be self-evident as they will be the same information that we covered in ad setup. Advertising reports we'll get to later.

In this screenshot we are looking at a sponsored category campaign that I have named "Piano Book Categories Ad". In the left column you will see a list of all the categories that are being targeted, along with ASINs if you added them together in the same campaign. I prefer to keep campaign types separate so will use another campaign for targeting ASINs. Either way, they will all look the same, the only differences are what you see in the left column: keywords, categories and products.

Automatic Targeting

Auto ads will be slightly different because we do not get to choose products or keywords. In the targeting tab for an auto campaign you might see four match types. These were discussed in the chapter "Sponsored Product Ads". Note in the image below these are called "Automatic targeting defaults". Amazon now call them "Automatic targeting groups".

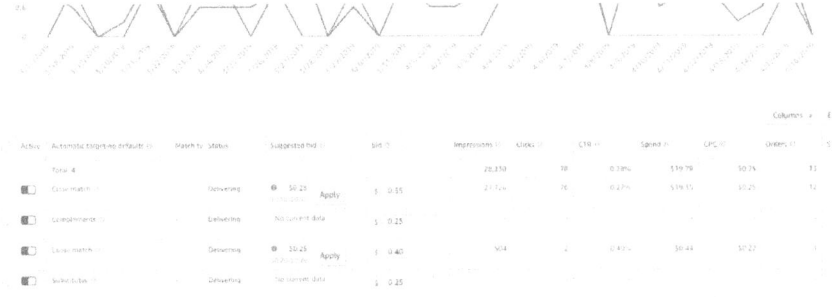

Optimising Campaigns

The ultimate goal is to make a profit from our campaigns. Everyone has different ideas about how to measure profit. I don't care too much about running every campaign with quick profit in mind. If you are in this for the long haul and you believe you write good books that people want to read, then every sale is helping you towards your goal, even if you spend more on advertising than you make in return, to an extent.

It's sometimes very difficult for people to be realistic. This isn't because they are in denial, it's because they lack experience. When I first started out in business, over thirty five years ago, I thought I knew what people wanted, just like we all do. It turns out the world does not work the way we think it does. Unfortunately it takes a very long while to learn this lesson. It's not arrogance, it's ignorance. Most of us suffer from it. We apply our own version of common sense to problems: unfortunately people do not buy what they actually need, they buy what they "think" they need, or more realistically, they just buy what they want. This will probably never change. This applies to "how-to" books and retail goods more so than it does with fiction books, however, fiction writers can still learn a lot from this because book covers, descriptions, advertising copy, reader demographics, habits and trends all play a part in how well something sells.

For non-fiction "how-to" books, it will be very difficult to rise above bullshit and outrageously hyped sales copy. Take two book titles ...

1. "How to improve your piano playing in under a year with methods that work"
2. "How to play piano from beginner to pro in under 7 days - Proven and Guaranteed"

We'll assume the book descriptions follow with sales copy similar to the titles. The first one is realistic, the second one is full of hype and factually impossible. I can almost guarantee that book 2 with all the hype will massively outsell the realistic book. I won't bore you with pretending I understand the psychology: most people will think "bullshit," yet buy it anyway. It's just how it is.

Fiction suffers similarly in that people when looking for a particular type of book, have a certain expectation. This is why we have to fall in line with these expectations, if we don't, then people pass us by. You must accept and realise this when you are writing your descriptions and design your book covers. Being unique doesn't make you stand out and get noticed, it makes you stand out to be ignored. Of course there will always be instances where this goes against the norm, but generally speaking, it's always best to stick with current trends.

OK, back to profit and the point I was getting at before I sidetracked. With the two non-fiction books above, the hyped one will very likely sell more. The other will build you a loyal audience. As long as you are sure that your book is good and realistic, it can build you a loyal fan base. Profit is not always about how quickly you can turn sales around, it's about investing in the future of your business. Whether you like it or not, being an author is being in business if you have any hopes of it becoming your living.

We can't put a number on how much this investment is worth. As mentioned above, we might be wrong: our books might not be as good as we think they are. We might also have a very limited budget. The point is this: if you are breaking even, or just losing a bit of money, then don't think that your ad campaigns are failing. You will figure out over time whether or not you are managing to build a loyal fan-base, at which point you can still run ads at break even if need be because you will eventually be making sales from your loyal readers and reputation. Obviously it's far better to profit from ads as well, and indeed it's the goal we are aiming for. Just remember to weigh up the pros and cons as things progress.

Understanding your Campaign Metrics

Before we can see how well our ads are doing and figure out how to improve them, we need to understand the metrics that we see in the dashboard. This is all of the information we have to work with. It's all we get, so the more we understand it, the better we will be able to work smarter.

Impressions

An impression is a count of your ad being displayed or triggered. If somebody searches for one of your keywords it counts as an impression. It is not the amount of times people typed that search term into Amazon's search bar, it's just the amount of times your ad got triggered. If you are showing 1000 impressions for one of your keywords, it means your ad got triggered 1000 times. This might only be a fraction of the amount of times the search term was actually used, you may have only won the bid 10% of the time.

An impression for a keyword targeted ad does not always show up only in the search results page. It can also show up on a detail page in the sponsored carousel. For example, if I am bidding for the keyword "how to play piano," I might not win the bid if somebody types that into search. What might happen, however, is the searcher clicks on another book that shows up in search results. This keyword will also have some influence on what ads get shown in the sponsored carousel, so your ad could potentially show up there instead of the search results page. Unfortunately Amazon does not give us this information in any of the reports so we don't know how often it happens. Just be aware of it.

Another thing to realise with impressions is this. An ad triggered and displayed does not mean that anybody actually looked at it. An impression is just an impression, it means your ad showed up. That could mean right at the bottom of the search results page. Many people searching on Amazon will click on one of the top few search results without scrolling down to the bottom of the page. A lot of searches don't even result in the page being scrolled down as far as the middle. If you are at the bottom of the page but the searcher clicks on the top result, then you will get an impression but not an actual view.

Product and category targeted ads will work similar. An impression will count when you show up on the sponsored carousel. A lot of the time, however, Amazon will show two rows of sponsored carousels on the detail page: one somewhere below the book description or below the also-boughts, and sometimes another near the bottom of the detail page. The same problem can apply: not everybody will scroll down to the bottom of the page, they will either hit the back button or click on one of the books in the carousels near the top.

An impression on the carousel is counted when your book is actually shown. At the top right of a carousel you will see "page 1 of ..." depending on how many page scrolls it contains ads for. If you are on page 5 of the carousel then an impression will only count when somebody scrolls along as far as page 5.

This isn't always a bad thing because people that click the first thing they see are usually not quite ready to buy. This can mean that further along the scroll page will get you fewer impressions but potentially a better sales possibility.

Clicks

I'm sure I don't need to explain this one but just in case, it's the amount of times somebody actually clicked on your ad.

CTR

CTR means click through rate. It's the ratio of clicks to impressions measured as a percentage. If you get an average 1 click for every 100 impressions, your CTR will be 1%. It's reasonable to expect much lower than this though. Obviously the higher the better but CTRs of 0.05% to 0.3% are quite common.

Spend

This is the total amount you have spent on clicks. If you get 10 clicks at an average of 0.20c then the spend will be $2.00.

CPC

This is the cost per click average.

Orders

Most of the time people will buy a single book, therefore *orders* will be approximately the amount of books sold. If however somebody clicks on one of your ads and ends up purchasing two or more of your books at the same time - this will count as a single order.

Sales

This is the total amount for sales. It does not account for royalties or ad spend, it's the amount your book sold for. If you sell ten books priced at $4.99 then the sales will be $49.90. It does not take into account borrows for Kindle Unlimited, nor refunds but will remove purchase cancellations made within 72 hours or payment failures. Depending on the country you are in, the sales amount may or may not include VAT or sales tax.

ACOS

ACOS is Advertising Cost of Sales and is simply the percentage of sales that was spent on ads. If your total ad spend is $10 and your sales total is $100 then your ACOS will be 10%. If sales are $50 and ad spend is $100 then your ACOS will be 200%.

Trying to get an accurate representation of your actual profit from ad campaigns is close to impossible unless you know exactly where every sale is coming from. Amazon does not give us this information. If you get most of your royalties from Kindle borrows then things are even harder to estimate.

Just remember, ACOS uses sales total, not royalties. If you only sell ebooks with a 70% royalty then things are simple. An ACOS of approximately 70% will be your break even point. I say approximate because this doesn't account for potential refunds nor the download fee.

If you sell paperbacks then your royalty might be 60% - print costs. If you sell a paperback for $8.99 with printing costs of $2.15 then your royalty will be 8.99 x 60% - 2.15 = 3.24. To work out the equivalent ACOS we need to work out our royalty compared to the selling price. We can do it like this:

(Royalty / sales price) x 100 so for the example above ...

(3.24 / 8.99) x 100 = 36.04

Therefore our break even ACOS for this paperback will be 36.04%.

Only you can work out what you think this figure should be because everybody's typical sales will be very different. For me personally, my ebook to paperback ratio is around 70/30 and I don't do much with Kindle borrows. If I see an ACOS of around 50% I will say that is roughly my break even. I don't care that it isn't accurate and I don't waste much time trying to calculate it anything more than a very rough estimation. If on the other hand I was spending thousands of dollars per month on advertising, then I would pay a lot more attention to this and try to get a far closer estimation of how well my ads are performing.

Monitoring Ad Campaigns

Once we have a basic understanding of these metrics, we can then begin to monitor our ads to see what works, what doesn't, and what can be improved or abandoned. The biggest problem we have to deal with is that ads can be unpredictable and inconsistent. Add to that, most of the reporting can be delayed. What this means in reality is we need to let things run for a while before we can make any decisions. There is no time frame for this, it depends on how many impressions, clicks and sales you are getting.

You will obviously need to draw some lines. If for instance you run an ad that is getting thousands of impressions with a lot of expensive clicks but no orders, then you might need to react quickly. If it isn't breaking the bank then still consider letting it run for at least four or five days minimum just in case it is working but the delayed reporting isn't yet showing sales. If on the other hand you have a very limited budget and this is looking like a potential disaster for you, then think about pausing the ad or lowering the bid. Never end an ad unless you are certain it's a disaster. Pausing or lowering the bid will allow you to start it up again if need be.

Above everything else, there are a few important rules that you need to adhere to.

1: Keep a log of every change you make, along with the date.

2: Never make more than one change at a time within a campaign, other than perhaps bid changes. Leave things for at least two weeks before changing them again. Why? Results are rarely instant. If you increase a bid, you might not see a change in the reports for a few days to a week. If you change more than one thing at a time then you have no idea what caused the change in the reports.

3: Never make a change in one campaign that can get offset by a change in another. For example, if two campaigns are bidding for the same category, product or keyword then they might compete or affect each other. If you change one, then leave the other as it is unless you have an objective reason to do so. As above, leave things for at least a few weeks.

4: If you use ad copy then don't use the exact same text in each campaign. For example, if I am running four campaigns for a single book - one for each manual targeting type and an auto targeting - then change the text in each one just slightly and keep a log of which ad text belongs to which ad campaign. It can be as little as a comma change or single word. This is not about testing ad copy, that's a different subject all together, although you could do this here if you wanted to. Let me elaborate ...

It's easy to get lazy or impatient. You may decide to run four separate campaigns for the same book as mentioned above. If you use the exact same ad copy for each one of them, then you have no way of knowing which ad is showing when you are looking through the Amazon website, which, by the way, you should do often. Optimising our ads goes beyond what we see in the dashboard. Quite often we will want to browse through the Amazon pages to see when and where our ad is showing up and what other authors we're showing up against. One tiny change in each ad will allow us to figure this out. For an example, let's say we see one of our ads repeatedly showing up right alongside other books that are completely non-related to ours. We might decide to use a negative keyword for that author or particular product page / category. We might also decide the opposite and see a potential for increasing bids. Knowing where the ad is coming from will allow us to make changes in the right places.

There is also another reason to use different ad copy, different from the reason above. We might just be testing different ad copy to see which performs better. This will often be very different ad copy for each campaign. This is a better strategy to use but takes more time and thought. Either way, as long as each ad is different, and you are keeping a record of it, then you will be able to know what ads are showing up.

One could argue that ad copy should be tested while all else is equal. For instance, an auto ad doesn't necessarily compare to a category targeted ad. This is possibly true and in an ideal test situation, this is what we would take into account. Personally I wouldn't worry about it because Amazon advertising isn't geared up for proper A/B testing and too many other variables could skew results. For manual keyword bidding, however, we can often expect a higher click through rate compared to other campaign types because the keywords are, or at least should be, better targeted and likely to be more relevant.

There is no single method for optimising campaigns. Each book, the genre, the competition involved - can all change the way we react and refine things. Unfortunately you need to figure these things out for yourself and much of it comes from pure experimentation. For the rest of this book I will show a bunch of examples of things I will look out for in a campaign. Learn by example as they say.

Analysing and Refining Campaigns 1

When we analyse our campaigns we need to dig deep. It's OK to look at an overall campaign's performance to see if we are making or losing money with the campaign as a whole, but often we will have multiple targets inside that can be varying massively. Another thing to be aware of is the scaling on the charts. Things can look very different in graphical form and force us to panic and make changes too quickly. Take a look at the images below, sometimes things look worse than they actually are.

The lines on the charts will jump around somewhat because they use a dual vertical axis with different scales. You can however hover the mouse over any point in the chart to bring up a little data window. See image below.

As you can see here, although spend is above the sales line, we aren't spending more than we are making in sales. Always hover over the lines when you want to check, you can easily find that the lines will switch if you change the date range or choose a different metric.

You can display a date range of up to 90 days in the chart with daily increments. Anything over this will divide the chart by month, with two choices, either "year to date" or "lifetime. It's a shame we can't choose more custom date ranges but that's what we have to live with. Hopefully one day in the future they'll increase the range, I won't hold my breath though.

Using a date range of 90 days can be useful but can also get messy and hard to decipher. The following image shows how we can get a rough idea of what's going on and is useful if we want to hone in and hover over specific dates.

However, if we use the monthly view (year to date or lifetime) then it's easier to spot trends that are not so clear with the detailed view.

We can see quite clearly what is going on from month to month. What's more important is that in the last month (in the above example) we can spot quite easily that spend is rising while sales don't seem to have moved. Again, don't take much notice of the distance between the lines, what we are concerned with here is that the spend is rising but sales aren't. If we hover over the chart we can see what the data points are for each month.

I've pieced together the image above so don't waste time trying to get your dashboard to show multiple data points at the same time, it can't be done. The thing to notice here is don't try to interpret charts at a glance. The spend and sales for January are very different, but the two lines almost meet, while the opposite is true for April.

It's good to spend time studying the chart data but the real detail is in the tables. We can view them by clicking on the "Targeting" tab from within the campaign (don't forget, these tabs have now been moved to the left side column).

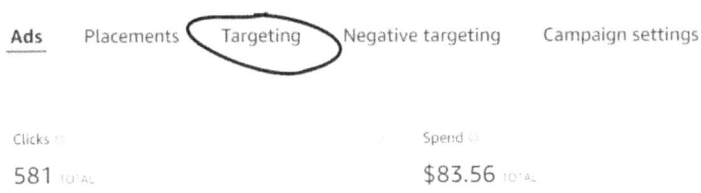

This is where we need to be looking most of the time. Let's take a look at the campaign shown in the previous image as it might need some work if the spend is rising above sales. It is a sponsored category campaign that I haven't paid enough attention to, so now is a good time to try fixing it.

This campaign started on Jan 12th which is beyond the 90 day timeline in the dashboard so the following image has been created in Google sheets. Ignore the numbers on the axis, I've altered the scale so that it makes more sense visually.

In the first two weeks, I was a bit hasty with bid adjustments. On 16th Jan I raised the bids around 0.05c on three categories that were looking good. This was when category targeting was newly introduced and very low bids of 5c to 7c were getting clicks and impressions. On Jan 27th I paused 35 (of 40) categories that didn't look like they were working. To be honest I didn't give them enough chance but the reason I paused them was because it was competing with another campaign and didn't "feel" like they were going to do very well. Here's the metrics for a selection of some of the ones that I paused. In hindsight I would have left them running a bit longer, for no other reason than the low bid prices. Either way, these particular categories weren't what I would have considered high relevance for the book.

Bid	Impressions	Clicks	CTR	Spend	CPC	Orders	Sales
	897,483	773	0.09%	$96.41	$0.12	41	
$ 0.07	9,426	2	0.02%	$0.08	$0.04	-	
$ 0.07	8,984	4	0.04%	$0.15	$0.04		
$ 0.07	8,644	6	0.07%	$0.34	$0.06	1	
$ 0.07	7,082	2	0.03%	$0.04	$0.02	-	
$ 0.07	6,838	5	0.07%	$0.16	$0.03	-	
$ 0.07	6,772	2	0.03%	$0.09	$0.05		
$ 0.07	3,664	4	0.11%	$0.16	$0.04		
$ 0.07	3,170	3	0.09%	$0.06	$0.02	-	
$ 0.07	2,555	3	0.12%	$0.11	$0.04	-	
$ 0.07	2,332	1	0.04%	$0.02	$0.02	-	
$ 0.07	2,215					-	
$ 0.07	1,902	1	0.05%	$0.02	$0.02	-	

Roughly two weeks in from the start of the campaign it appeared to be losing momentum gradually. On the 28th Jan I increased the bids again on two of the categories by 5c and 10c. The following image shows a downward trend appearing within the first two weeks, but then picking up again after this second round of bid increases. I also lowered the bid on one of the other categories.

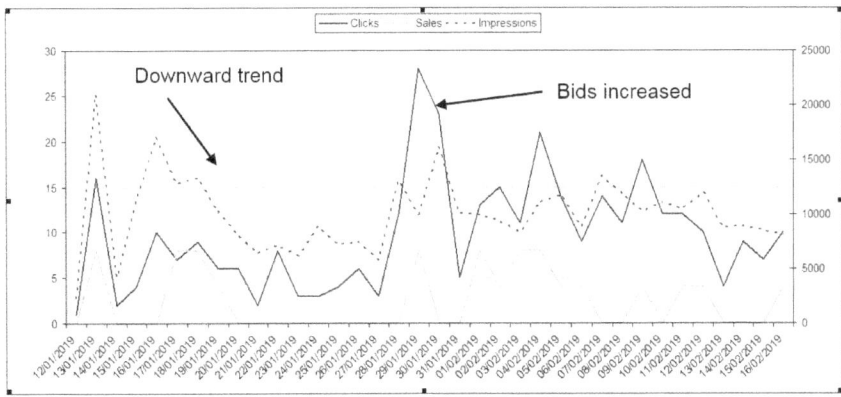

We can see here a large jump in impressions and clicks from the date of this bid increase and sales start to happen again a day later on the 29th, after an eleven day lull.

To summarise so far, for the first two weeks I raised bids on categories that looked like they were doing well but had started to drop. I Then lowered the bid back down on one that didn't improve after raising the bid. Paused all the categories that wasn't performing very well. That was a lot of changes for just two weeks, normally I would let things run a little longer.

Over the next six weeks I let the campaign run with no changes until 17th March. In that time, clicks and spend were falling slowly. I decided to increase bids again.

	Clicks	Spend	CPC	Impressions	Sales
	357 TOTAL	$38.63 TOTAL	$0.11 AVERAGE	349,062 TOTAL	$75.81 TOTAL

The table below shows the metrics for the five enabled categories between Feb 1st and March 17th.

	Impressions	Clicks	CTR	Spend	CPC	Orders	Sales	ACOS
	349,062	357	0.10%	$38.63	$0.11	19	$75.81	50.96%
Cat 1	157,632	166	0.12%	$16.91	$0.10	8	$31.92	52.98%
Cat 2	135,818	78	0.06%	$7.73	$0.10	2	$7.98	96.87%
Cat 3	54,665	98	0.18%	$12.60	$0.13	7	$27.95	45.11%
Cat 4	16,360	14	0.09%	$1.32	$0.09	2	$7.98	16.54%
Cat 5	4,587	1	0.02%	$0.07	$0.07	-	-	

Here are the bid adjustments I made.

Category 1: 20c to 25c
Category 2: 17c to 10c
Category 3: 20c to 25c
Category 4: 17c to 10c
Category 5: Paused

So far the data in the previous charts show the total for the whole campaign. Here is what each of these targeted categories look like individually for clicks and sales. Impressions have also been dropping across all of the targeted categories.

To get a timeline view for individual categories, we use the filter. Just copy the category name and paste it into the filter and hit the Enter key on your keyboard, or click the filter button.

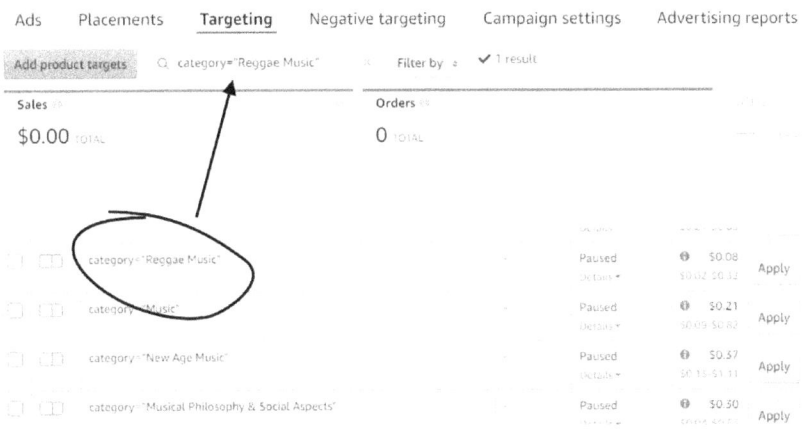

Category 1: Clicks and sales have been falling but still made two sales in March so I think it could do better and raised the bid. 20c to 25c doesn't sound much but it's still a 25% increase.

Category 2: Clicks are going up but no sales since 17th Feb so it doesn't look promising. It's had sales so I didn't pause it, just lowered the bid for now.

Impressions	Clicks	Sales	Spend	CPC
135,818 TOTAL	78 TOTAL	$7.98 TOTAL	$7.73 TOTAL	$0.10 AVERAGE

Category 2

Category 3: Still making regular sales but the clicks are dropping, along with impressions. This feels like a good one so I raised the bid from 20c to 25c.

Impressions	Clicks	Sales	Spend	CPC
54,665 TOTAL	98 TOTAL	$27.93 TOTAL	$12.60 TOTAL	$0.13 AVERAGE

Category 3

Category 4: Similar to category 2, just a couple of sales in Feb but still getting clicks. Bid lowered for now.

Impressions	Clicks	Sales	Spend	CPC
16,360 TOTAL	14 TOTAL	$7.98 TOTAL	$1.32 TOTAL	$0.09 AVERAGE

Category 4

Category 5: This one just isn't happening so it has been paused.

Impressions	Clicks	Sales	Spend	CPC
4,587 TOTAL	1 TOTAL	$0.00 TOTAL	$0.07 TOTAL	$0.07 AVERAGE

Category 5

The idea now should be to monitor the changes over the next two weeks or so. Despite all my preaching, I made more changes three days later. To be honest I don't know why I did it, I've been experimenting and trying to optimise my campaigns lately but obviously wasn't paying attention to detail. I made two mistakes. First, I raised the bids again on three of the categories. Second, I switched on bid+ (now replaced by dynamic bidding). Raising the bids twice is forgivable. Switching on Bid+ was stupid because now it will be difficult to know what effect it has, the reporting is not great in this area.. Oh well, silly me!

Here is what I did, all on 20th March.

Category 1: Raised bid from 0.25c to 0.35c
Category 3: Raised bid from 0.25c to 0.35c
Category 4: Raised bid from 0.10c to 0.35c
Enabled Bid+

As you can see, there wasn't any strategy. It's only now that I'm looking at my logs and writing this down at this very moment, the word "haphazard" is springing to mind. Anyway, if you're paying attention, you'll have noticed that for category 4, I lowered the bid on the 17th and then raised it again on the 20th. This is because of gut feeling. This targeted category, although not performing very well, I just think it should because it is very relevant to the book. Anyway, let's have a look to see the effect of raising the bids, here's the 90 day chart again.

We can see here that it has certainly had an effect. Spend has increased and it looks like a few extra sales have happened as a result. It might be useful now to zoom in and have a closer look. Let's have a look at two weeks either side of the 20th March. Note: sometimes I switch between metrics to get different ideas. The following two charts are using clicks and sales because it gives a clearer picture in this instance.

It's not huge, but certainly an improvement. We can dig even deeper and look at the effect this has had on the four categories individually. As a reminder, since the start of the campaign I have paused most of the targeted categories. For the past four weeks these are the only categories still running. Let's take a look at each of them from our bid changes at 28th Jan to April 24th (today's date as I'm writing).

Category 1: This one did not get any bid changes on the 28th Jan. From around the 12th Feb it starts to drop off. Bid increased 20th March and then spend starts to go up and a few more sales. Problem here is there's not enough happening to know whether these last few sales are as a result of the bid increase. Looking at this timeline might suggest that these sales could have happened anyway. From the 10th of April the spend is going up but no more orders. Not shown in this image are clicks which are going down from the 10th of April which means my CPC is going up. I will probably go back to a low bid for this category and check again in a few weeks.

Category 2: From the 28th Jan, spend was going up as expected. Two sales follow over the next three weeks and then no more. Spend continues to move up. This is why I dropped the bid on the 17th march. One sale on the 23th March and another on the 17th April, which is a paperback so ignore the large spike, it's just a single sale. I'll probably keep the bid where it is as it's only $0.10c.

Category 3: This one is looking much better. Raising the bid on the 28th Jan didn't have a great deal of impact on spend but sales are trickling fairly regularly. The spend starts to go up after the next bid increase and sales continue. I like the look of this one, even though the CPC is higher, it does appear to be working. For now, I'll ignore how profitable is (or isn't) and keep monitoring. I might even increase the bid further still.

Category 4: Everything tells us this just isn't working. I really should just pause it, however, like I mentioned earlier, this category should be the most relevant of them all. Sometimes our logic defies us and we should just give in to defeat but I'm not going to go without a fight on this. Maybe this category is just far more competitive than I realise. Maybe I should research it more. Maybe I'm just wrong and should ignore "gut feelings" and get over it. Here is what I'm going to do instead, one last attempt. I'll very likely lose money but I need to satisfy my curiosity: I might even learn something. I'm going to bid much higher...

Note: Before I carry on, I should mention Bid+ (now dynamic bidding). Although I enabled this at the same time as the bid increases shown in the charts above, I have ignored it for now. Looking through my reports (although they aren't very detailed) I can't see any evidence that this has helped or hindered. So far it has created 13 impressions and no clicks. For the rest of this experiment I will be disabling it again, starting right now.

Okay, back to bidding. These are the suggested bids for this category:

Low: $0.38
Median: $0.78
High: $1.64

Most people will tell you to ignore the suggested bids. I completely agree with them. Why? Because if you monitor them, you'll realise they continually change. So far I have found no pattern, and to be honest, I won't try hard looking for one. I think allowing them to guide your bid amount is a recipe for disaster. I'm sure there's something in them, I doubt they are random numbers, but it's also likely Amazon only display them just in order to get us to spend more. To give you an example, here are some of the suggested bids for this single category.

	Low	Median	High
16-Mar	0.39	0.77	1.67
18-Mar	0.41	0.82	1.77
19-Mar	0.39	0.81	1.89
21-Mar	0.4	0.78	1.92
22-Mar	0.35	0.69	2
24-Mar	0.35	0.73	2.09
26-Mar	0.42	0.75	1.85
29-Mar	0.46	0.78	1.97
02-Apr	0.53	0.84	1.83
06-Apr	0.54	0.99	2.33
08-Apr	0.58	1.01	2.58
09-Apr	0.52	0.98	2.28
10-Apr	0.53	0.98	2.47
13-Apr	0.52	0.96	2.08
17-Apr	0.43	0.8	1.69
18-Apr	0.36	0.78	1.71

April 8th, the suggested high bid is $2.58. Compare that to three weeks earlier: on the 16th March it was $1.67. If I go back to Jan and Feb, they were all much lower. The only pattern here is the average tends to increase over time. Either way, if we rely on it, eventually we will collectively bid ourselves out of the market.

Here's what I'm going to do. I am going to bid $2.60. I'm already getting nervous thinking about it so I've capped the daily budget at $30.

I'll let it run for two weeks and see what happens. I'll be keeping a very watchful eye on it and if it looks like I'm heading for disaster, I'll bottle it and pull out. We shall see. This is now happening in real time as I write this book so I'll come back here and update on its progress.

I'm also going to increase the bid for category 3, as it looks kind of promising, and let it run for two weeks. The suggested low bid is 0.55. I'm going to set it at 0.45.

To summarise this campaign so far. Only two of the targeted categories have shown any real promise so I've increased the bids on them. All the others have now been paused or had their bids lowered again.

High Bid Experiment Result

I said I might cut the high bid experiment short, and I did, after four and a half days. I didn't bottle it exactly; I said I might learn something, and that's what happened. First let's take a look at the screenshots, I'll add a bunch of them so that you can see the metrics for yourself and one over the whole month so you can see the jump it created.

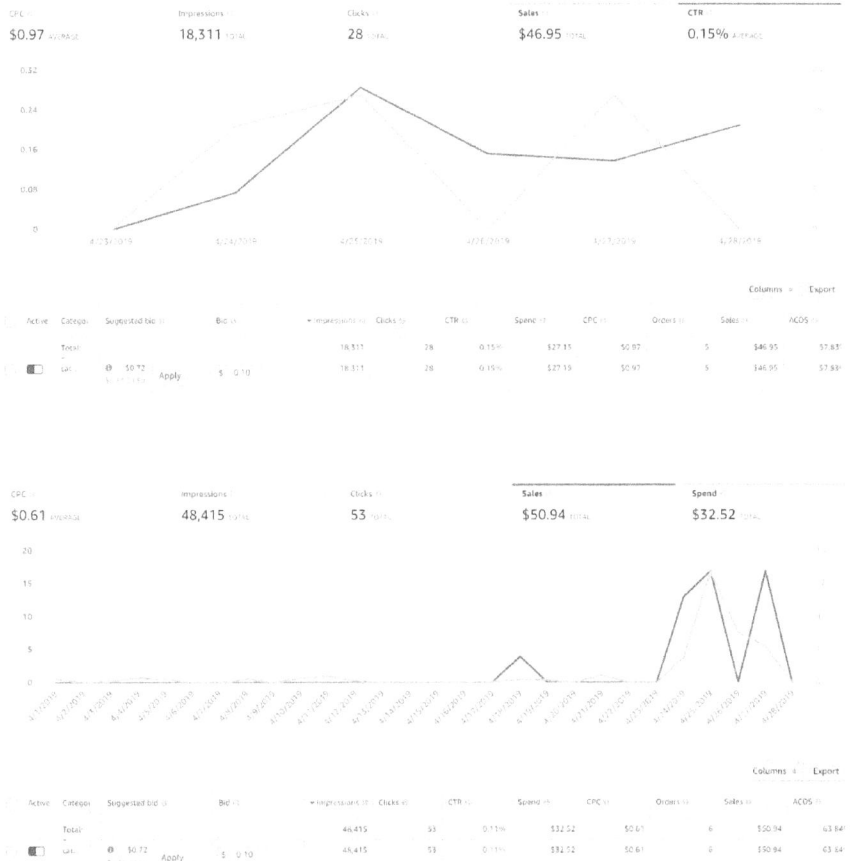

At first glimpse it looks like it's doing quite well. The problem is the sales are mostly paperback so looks can be deceiving. The royalties on those sales add up to approximately $14 so the actual ACOS is over 200%. Obviously I did not give it enough time to get an accurate account of that but here's the problem and these are the types of things we need to look out for.

Clicks went up for the first two days and then started dropping. The impressions started dropping two days after that. This is a possible sign (not definite) that the algorithms aren't feeling enthusiastic about this ad. When an ad is working well, the impressions should stay around the same or possibly go up. My thoughts here are that for the high bid, the amount of impressions and clicks I was getting, the algorithms felt it should be doing better. This is all gut feeling so far.

Throughout these four days I was regularly checking the top 100 books in this category and noticed that I wasn't showing up at all on many of them. For some of them I was way down from the top position, on the third or fourth scroll page on the carousel. Only on very few pages was I showing anywhere near, or at, the top position.

Straight away we can learn from this that the highest bid doesn't guarantee the fist position. I can't be certain but I think it highly probable I had the highest bid among all other advertisers. At worst, I would probably have been in the top five.

Here's the interesting part. For nearly every book page where I wasn't showing up, these books were not what I would call particularly relevant to my book. After a browse through the actual category and the associated top 100 on the Amazon site, very few of the books listed were particularly relevant to mine. Remember back in the chapter "running and optimising your ads" where we looked at the "Country Music" section mostly full of fiction? That's similar to what is happening in my targeted category. It's not full of fiction books but it is full of books from a similar, but not exactly relevant sub-category.

So why did I not notice this before? Because this same category in the Kindle store contains books I would expect to see. Category ads target mostly book (paperback) categories. I simply hadn't done my homework here and made assumptions that the Kindle categories would pretty much reflect the book categories. Not in this instance it didn't.

Should I have kept this running longer to be sure? Maybe. The thing is, sales were coming, CPC was not going down but impressions and clicks were. Unless everything moved in the opposite direction, my ACOS would probably remain around, or above 200% ... probably.

At some point in the future I might decide to conduct the experiment again. However, this time I'll first spend more time double checking relevancy and maybe try the high bid experiment on something that is already working well. I think this will bring more interesting results.

Category 3 bid increase

Here is the result of raising the bid to 0.45c for category 3. As we can see, sales and spend have both gone up.

Long story short, I had to take a break from writing this book at the end of April so I couldn't get this data from the dashboard. The graph above was created with Google sheets using my saved reports. Not a problem, that's why we download and save our reports. Reason I'm telling you this is because it's now almost the end of October so I can show you a bit more info about this category.

From the time of the bid increase on the 24th of April I have left this campaign almost untouched. On the 1st of June I dropped the bid to 0.42c. Also on the 14th July I went through the search reports and looked for some ASINs were getting clicks but very few or no sales. I added them to the negative products. The image below shows the timeline for the whole year for this single category (not the entire campaign).

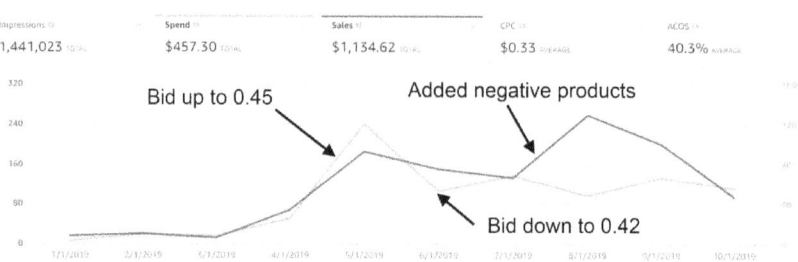

I'll be honest, during my break I had a lot going on and wasn't paying a great deal of attention to my ads. With that said, I'm unsure why I dropped the bid to 0.42. It's hard to tell with a monthly graph whether the slight bid drop or adding negative products have made much difference, although it does look like it's probable. To be certain I would have to dig deep into the reports and maybe look at the daily data two weeks each side of the changes. Even then, ad campaigns do fluctuate so the main thing we are looking for is a reasonably consistent profit. What we can tell from looking at the two graphs above is that since upping the bid to 0.45 this category has jumped up significantly and remained fairly consistent with very few further changes.

Although it does look like it's dropping off this month I won't panic just yet. There is still two days left until the end of the month so that sales line could still move up a bit. I will only worry if that line continues to move downward over the next month. The ACoS has moved up and down over this period but overall the campaign has stayed in profit and click cost remains steady at around 0.33c per click average. In case you are curious, here's the year for ACoS and CPC. I've included the ACoS percentages on the timeline.

Impressions	Spend	Sales	CPC	ACOS
1,441,023	$457.30	$1,134.62	$0.33	40.3%

17%   49%   65%   37%   64%   35%   51%   18%   33%   59%

Campaign Strategies

The last few chapters took a detailed look at how I might analyse and try to refine a category targeted campaign. Whether we are working with targeted products, categories or manual keyword campaigns, the same principles apply so there is no need to repeat it for each campaign type. The only difference you will see is what's in the tables. For products it will be a list of ASINs and for keywords it will be a keyword list.

Generally, we want to run at least one of each campaign type for each book we are advertising. In most cases the best performing, and most efficient of them will be the manual keyword targeted campaigns. We never know, however, what will work best. Manual keywords are most likely to produce the best results, but far from guaranteed. Competition, relevance and many other factors might make one campaign work better than another. Sometimes it just happens and we have no idea why.

Setting out a strategy to begin with is the best way to refine our ads over time. Nobody, unless incredibly lucky, starts out with highly efficient campaigns. We get to this point over time by examining and refining as we go. The good thing right now is Amazon are making life much easier for us to implement a plan. Things have changed quite a lot, even in the seven or eight weeks since I started writing this book. Best of all, we now have the long awaited search term reports. We'll take a look at these a bit later to see what we can learn from them. They are a game changer which now gives us the opportunity to dig deep and refine our campaigns more effectively.

As mentioned, we never really know what will work best so we have to wait things out and adapt over time. For each book, we should start with one of each Sponsored ad type.

1: Auto Targeting
2: Category Targeting
3: Individual Product Targeting
4: Manual Keyword

We can, if we wish, combine category ads and individual products in the same campaign. I advise against this because it makes things more difficult to refine and measure. Better off keeping things separate.

Probably the two most important campaigns will be the individual product and the manual keywords because these are the ones that are highly targeted. The other two, Auto and Category, are what we use to make discoveries. It's also possible that the latter two could turn out to be our best performers. If this happens then we just let them carry on working for us. Until these ads have run for a few months we'll never know. In the meantime, we just let them all run and wait for them to collect data.

The bidding strategies for each campaign will need to be experimented with because to some extent they will be competing with each other. I say "to some extent" because there are too many variables to really say they compete. For example, somebody might use a search term on Amazon, click on a search result and end up on some book's detail page that could trigger any one of your ads if the criteria fits. This doesn't necessarily mean it will be the campaign or ad with the highest bid that gets triggered. The only way you can find out is to let them all run for a while and check the reports. Generally speaking, if relevancy is good across all campaigns, the one with the higher bid will get shown the most.

This should become evident once a campaign has been running for at least a few weeks. Let's say you bid all four campaigns at 0.25c for each keyword, product etc. If after a week or so you find that the category ads are getting all of the clicks and nothing is happening with the rest of them, try increasing the bids on the others; but don't drop the bid on the one that is working, at least not straight away. If something is working at the start then it's best left alone until it has run for a while.

If you see the campaigns with the increased bids start to work, it could be that they just needed to have higher bids. If however you find that at the same time the category ad starts to slow up, then it's likely they are affecting each other. Unfortunately we just can't get this kind of information quickly, we have to wait for things to happen and then check the reports.

All we are trying to do is let ads run and collect data that gives us ideas about what works and what doesn't. Over time we then use this data to compile highly targeted keywords and individual product ads.

Once our ad campaigns have been running for a few weeks we can monitor and refine them as discussed in the chapter "Analysing and Refining Campaigns 1". In addition to this we will also be checking the search term reports to drill down and optimise our campaigns further.

Reports

Advertising reports are downloadable reports that can be opened up in a spreadsheet such as Excel or Google sheets etc. To get your reports, click on the "Advertising reports" tab from the dashboard (which is now available in the left hand column as discussed in the chapter "Dashboard Updates").

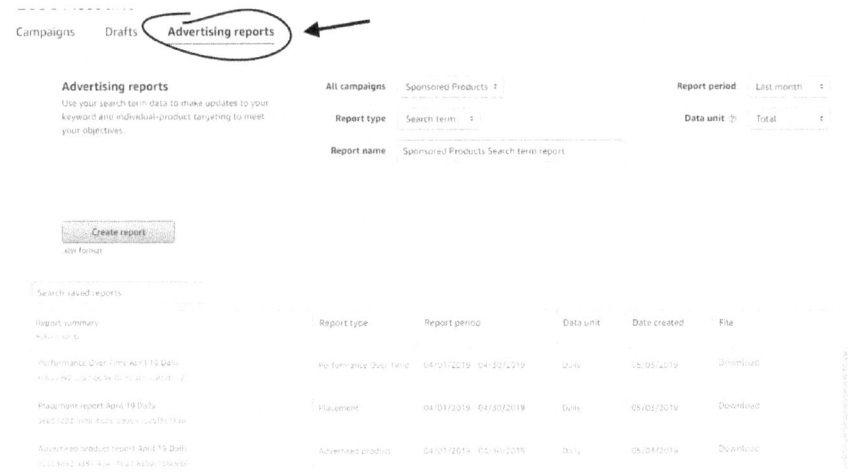

Let's quickly run through the options.

All Campaigns:

This button might give you a few options such as Product display ads, Sponsored brands or Sponsored products, depending on what account type you have. We're only talking about KDP accounts here and the only reports we are interested in for the purpose of this book are the Sponsored Products.

Report Type:

This button will let you choose the report type. Currently there are five options:

1: Search term
2: Targeting
3: Advertised product
4: Placement
5: Performance over time

The most important of them all is the search term report. I've not found much use for any of the others except for maybe the Placement reports, but to be honest, I don't use it much because it lacks a lot of important information like bid costs and dates that bids were changed. This is why we must always keep a log of our changes when we make them. If we don't, then the Placement reports become almost useless.

The only report I will talk about in this book is the search term report, it's the most useful.

With that said, every month you should download all five report types and save them. Don't take my word for how useful they are or not. You might prefer to look at spreadsheet data rather than the dashboard, in which case they may work better for you. For instance, targeting reports are almost a snapshot of what we see in the dashboard. If you want to view daily data further back than 90 days then you can get most of the info viewable from the dashboard if you've saved these reports.

Sometimes we also change the way we work, I might myself at a later date have a completely different way of working, so save them all every month just in case. Make a habit of it because we can only pull 60 days of previous data.

Report Name:
Name your report how you like. I personally name them by product type followed by the month and year. You'll want to keep

these reports and refer to them over time so it's always a good idea to name them in a way you can find them easily.

Report Period:

You can choose customised dates or use one of the presets. I always wait until at least a week into the month and then choose "Last month". This allows some overlap to deal with delays and reporting lag. Most of all it just keeps me organised by downloading reports in full months rather than date ranges which can get messy.

Data unit:

Two choices here. Daily or Total. Daily reports will show the data for each search term for each day of the month (or report period). Total reports will give the collated data per keyword and / or customer search term. I prefer daily reports because it gives a better representation of how targeting is working throughout the month and allows us to create more accurate timeline charts within Excel, if we wish to. Everything I talk about here will be with reference to daily reports.

The Search Term Report

Note: You should already have a basic understanding of using Excel. If not then now is the time to learn how to use functions like sort and filtering. There are plenty of good tutorials about this found for free the Internet so I won't be explaining any of that here. If you don't own Excel then you can use Google sheets or something like Libreoffice, both of which are free and will have plenty of tutorials available with a simple web search.

Once you have downloaded and opened up the search term report in Excel (or your preferred spreadsheet software) you will be presented with a list of all your campaigns and keywords that got clicks and / or sales. You will see many columns, most are self-evident, things like impressions, CPC, Match type etc. The one we are most interested in is the column titled "Customer Search Term". This tells us the actual keyword phrase that was used by the customer - or ASIN of the product page that had our ad displayed.

There are many ways you could use and interpret this data. I'll show you what I do. I look for two main things in this report. Search terms and ASINs that get repeated sales; and those that get clicks with no sales, or very few. The following image shows a small, very shrunken down, section of what some of this data will look like in the report.

	D	E	F	G	
cy	Campaign Name	Targeting	Match Type	Customer Search Term	Ir
	Book 1 Campaign Categories	category="Music Composition"	-	1118837428	
	Book 1 Campaign Categories	category="Piano"	-	9780470224212	
	Book 1 Campaign Categories	category="Blues Music"	-	1118900057	
	Book 1 Campaign Categories	category="Music Theory"	-	1615640495	
	Book 1 Campaign Products	asin="1118837428"	-	1118837428	
	Book 1 Campaign Products	asin="9780470224212"	-	9780470224212	
	Book 1 Campaign Products	asin="1118900057"	-	1118900057	
	Book 1 Campaign Products	asin="1615640495"	-	1615640495	
	Book 1 Campaign Keywords	Learn piano	BROAD	how to learn piano	
	Book 1 Campaign Keywords	Piano exercises	BROAD	piano exercises	
	Book 1 Campaign Keywords	Play piano	BROAD	how to play piano	
	Book 1 Campaign Keywords	Piano music theory	BROAD	music theory for piano	
	Book 1 Campaign Auto	*	-	piano for beginners	
	Book 1 Campaign Auto	*	-	piano for dummies	
	Book 1 Campaign Auto	*	-	1615640495	
	Book 1 Campaign Auto	*	-	1615640495	

The column "Campaign Name" shows a list of your advertising campaigns.

The "Targeting" Column shows what you are targeting, e.g., your keywords, categories and product ASINs that you are bidding for. Auto campaigns will just show an asterisk here as we're not targeting anything specific.

The "Match Type" columns will show the targeting type for manual keyword campaigns: Broad, phrase or exact.

The "Customer Search Term" column shows the actual search term that somebody typed into search, or the ASIN for the book whose detail page our ad was shown.

One of the first things you can do in this report is look for the ACoS column and sort by descending. This will bring all of the clicks with sales to the top of the spreadsheet. You can then look through the customer search terms column to see which terms or ASINs produced sales. You'll need to just browse through for yourself to get the idea, there is too much data in the spreadsheet to show here in a single image.

	L	M	N	
(CPC)	Spend	14 Day Total Sales	Total Advertising Cost of Sales (ACoS)	Total
$ 1.00	$ 3.98	$ 3.99	99.7494%	
$ 0.75	$ 0.75	$ 3.99	18.7970%	
$ 0.34	$ 0.67	$ 3.99	16.7920%	
$ 0.44	$ 1.31	$ 7.98	16.4160%	
$ 0.30	$ 0.60	$ 3.99	15.0376%	
$ 1.93	$ 1.93	$ 12.99	14.8576%	
$ 0.24	$ 0.48	$ 3.99	12.0301%	
$ 0.47	$ 0.47	$ 3.99	11.7794%	
$ 0.42	$ 0.42	$ 3.99	10.5263%	
$ 0.21	$ 0.42	$ 3.99	10.5263%	
$ 0.35	$ 0.35	$ 3.99	8.7719%	
$ 0.34	$ 0.34	$ 3.99	8.5213%	
$ 0.33	$ 0.33	$ 3.99	8.2707%	

This is a quick and easy way to find keywords and ASINs that are working. It won't, however, help us find those that aren't. To do this we need to sort the "customer search term" column. We need to look for groups of keywords and ASINs that have had more than just a few clicks. This might be the kind of data you will see in these three columns:

Customer Search Terms / Clicks / 14 Day Total orders

B000FC1JXA / 1 / 0
B003JMFDLW / 5 / 0
B004GEB6W2 / 1 / 0
B004N61A60 / 2 / 0
B004P1J8RQ / 7 / 0
B0062YCULK / 1 / 1
B006KM0IOA / 3 / 0
B0083V4C2A / 9 / 0
B00BFUORGC / 5 / 1
B00CD0L2I4 / 4 / 0
B00CLWUTWY / 1 / 0
B00CWR4ZQE / 2 / 0
B00DLYULBK / 8 / 0

You are going to find many unique keywords and ASINs with and without clicks and sales. We can't really garner much information from these other than look up some of those ASINs to make sure we're targeting the right kind of books. What we need to look for is groups of similar keywords and ASINs. If we have a bunch of them together then we know that our ad was shown repeatedly for those targets. Here's a few examples to demonstrate what I mean.

B0169MXCWA / 1 / 0
B017OBN7AW / 2 / 0
B017OBN7CK / 1 / 1
B017OBN7CK / 7 / 0
B017OBN7CK / 9 / 0
B017OBN7CK / 8 / 2
B017OBN7CK / 2 / 1
B017OBN7CK / 4 / 0
B017OBN7CK / 6 / 0
B017OBN7CK / 2 / 0
B017OBN7CK / 3 / 1
B017OBN7CK / 5 / 1
B017OBN7CK / 1 / 0
B017OBN7CK / 9 / 2
B074NCPHX2 / 1 / 0

In the above example we can see a group of the same ASIN "B017OBN7CK" with both clicks and sales. This is a good indicator that this ASIN is getting us some decent sales. We could add up the cost of the clicks and sales to decide what to do with it. We could decide to raise or lower the bid to see if we can make it work even better.

If, however, it looks something like this, we will see that it's getting clicks but no sales, or possibly not enough sales to make it worth continuing with.

B0169MXCWA / 1 / 0
B017OBN7AW / 2 / 0
B017OBN7CK / 1 / 0
B017OBN7CK / 7 / 0
B017OBN7CK / 9 / 0
B017OBN7CK / 8 / 1
B017OBN7CK / 2 / 0
B017OBN7CK / 4 / 0
B017OBN7CK / 6 / 0
B017OBN7CK / 2 / 0
B017OBN7CK / 3 / 0
B017OBN7CK / 5 / 0
B017OBN7CK / 1 / 0
B017OBN7CK / 9 / 0
B074NCPHX2 / 1 / 0

The above examples will be exactly the same for keywords, so may look like this:

Learn piano / 1 / 0
Piano exercises / 2 / 0
Piano for beginners / 1 / 0
Piano for beginners / 7 / 0
Piano for beginners / 9 / 0
Piano for beginners / 8 / 1
Piano for beginners / 2 / 0
Piano for beginners / 4 / 0
Piano for beginners / 6 / 0
Piano for beginners / 2 / 0
Piano for beginners / 3 / 0
Piano for beginners / 5 / 0
Piano for beginners / 1 / 0
Piano for beginners / 9 / 0
Piano scales / 1 / 0

There are a lot of things we can check throughout this report. If we see an ASIN or keyword that is getting many clicks but no sales then we should check them for ourselves on Amazon to make sure Amazon is throwing up relevant results. If my book is about piano but is getting shown repeatedly on an ASIN that is about playing Trombone, then I have a relevancy problem that needs to be taken care of, or I need to use those ASINs for negative targeting. Same with keywords. It doesn't always matter if we think a keyword should be relevant or not. If our book is about "piano for beginners" but when we type that into Amazon it brings up mostly results for piano sheet music ... Amazon has the relevancy wrong, but it's still wrong and we need to think about removing that keyword if it's getting clicks with no sales.

Another thing worth doing is sorting the "Clicks" and the "Spend" column. This might bring our attention to things we might otherwise miss. For example, earlier I said unique ASINs and keywords don't tell us much. Generally they should just be ignored until we have more data. Sorting by clicks and spend (descending), however, we might notice a unique ASIN or keyword with a lot of clicks or high spend but no sales. Things like this might be flaws in the data or one-off occurrences, but worth double checking that we aren't bidding too high, or perhaps just noting and keeping a watchful eye on. Never panic and just pause these kinds of things unless you are certain you don't want to bid on them. Sometimes a few more weeks of data can reveal much more.

There is no simple formula for figuring any of this out. All we can do is look at the data in the reports and just decipher things the best we can with the information we have. This is one of the reasons I prefer to use daily reports as they reveal a bit more of what is happening. For example, let's say we see something like the following in a 60 day daily report.

B017OBN7CK / 2 / 0
B017OBN7CK / 1 / 0
B017OBN7CK / 7 / 0
B017OBN7CK / 9 / 1
B017OBN7CK / 8 / 0
B017OBN7CK / 2 / 0
B017OBN7CK / 4 / 0
B017OBN7CK / 6 / 0
B017OBN7CK / 2 / 0
B017OBN7CK / 3 / 0
B017OBN7CK / 5 / 0
B017OBN7CK / 1 / 0
B017OBN7CK / 9 / 0
B017OBN7CK / 11 / 0
B017OBN7CK / 14 / 0
B017OBN7CK / 8 / 1
B017OBN7CK / 12 / 0
B017OBN7CK / 11 / 0
B017OBN7CK / 15 / 0
B017OBN7CK / 10 / 0
B017OBN7CK / 14 / 1
B017OBN7CK / 11 / 0

In a total report, this data might be all on one line within a given date range, something like this.

B017OBN7CK / 165 / 3

165 clicks with 3 sales could easily make us panic. Trouble is it doesn't tell us the full story. Just over halfway down we start to see an increase in clicks and then a sale followed by another sale a

few lines further down. This could be caused by a bid increase or change we have made somewhere, or it could even be Amazon is starting to give our ad some more visibility and moved it further up the page or into a better position on the sponsored carousel. It's entirely possible that if we leave this a week or so longer - it might start to look like this.

B017OBN7CK / 14 / 0
B017OBN7CK / 8 / 1
B017OBN7CK / 12 / 0
B017OBN7CK / 11 / 0
B017OBN7CK / 15 / 0
B017OBN7CK / 10 / 0
B017OBN7CK / 14 / 1
B017OBN7CK / 11 / 0
B017OBN7CK / 9 / 0
B017OBN7CK / 11 / 2
B017OBN7CK / 9 / 0
B017OBN7CK / 8 / 0
B017OBN7CK / 10 / 0
B017OBN7CK / 11 / 2
B017OBN7CK / 9 / 1
B017OBN7CK / 11 / 0

Which would give us this in total reports

B017OBN7CK / 173 / 7

Maybe not ideal but possibly still in profit with a sale approximately every 25 clicks. This kind of thing does sometimes happen and its why we need to sometimes wait a while before we take action.

Now that we know this ASIN is producing clicks and sales, we could try lowering or raising our bid to see what happens with it over the next few weeks. We might find that lowering the bid slightly will just bring the keyword / ASIN into profit by giving us a slightly lower CPC without losing clicks. On the other hand, we might find lowering the bid will see it producing fewer sales. We just can't know these things unless we try them. Raising the bid might seem counter-intuitive when an ad is working around break even. Our logic should tell us that if we force up our CPC then we'll just be paying more for the same clicks. The problem is we just don't know how Amazon's algorithms will react to a higher bid. We would assume that it will show the ad in a higher position. What we don't know is how that higher position will affect sales and change the potential buyers that see the ad and are more likely to buy our book. The only way we can find this out is by experimenting.

Analysing and Refining Campaigns 2

Once we have collected enough data in our search term reports, we should be able to compile a list of what is working and what isn't. We use this information to improve our ad campaigns. In an ideal world the search reports would give us more information. One such thing would be the ASIN of where our ad is shown with manual keyword campaigns. When somebody types something into the search bar at Amazon, this is what triggers the ad in our manual keyword campaigns. This doesn't mean the ad will only be shown in search results pages; it also influences what might show up in the sponsored carousel of detail pages. For example, I could type "learn how to play piano" into the search which then displays a bunch of books on the search results page. I could then click on one of these books (which is not my own) and be taken to that book's detail page. It's here that my ad might show up in the sponsored carousel. In other words even though I'm bidding on "learn how to play piano" it doesn't mean that every time I get a click, that click is coming from the search results pages. Manual keyword ads can also show up on detail pages of books that have related keywords which means these ads can also show up on pages where no search term was typed into the search bar.

Why does this matter? Because it might just be that this keyword is getting clicks but mostly showing up on another book's page. If we then target that particular book's ASIN in a product-targeting campaign, it might affect the performance of some keywords in our manual keyword targeted campaigns. We can get some clues by cross referencing various reports but in all honesty, it just makes things too complicated and impossible to analyse with any accuracy. Just be mindful of it. If we notice a sudden decline with a particular keyword then remember to correlate it with other changes you may have made in another campaign.

There is no single strategy for refining campaigns and making them profitable. A lot of advertisers will run many campaigns for the same book, sometimes hundreds, even thousands - and then weed out the ones that aren't working while paying attention to the ones that are. I personally don't like this method because it's too messy and hard to manage. We also have to adapt occasionally because the system changes often. The one thing to always remember, however, is quite simple: some things work well and some things don't. As simple and obvious as that sounds, it's easy to lose sight of but remains at the heart of everything we do to make our ads work. It's also dynamic: what doesn't work today might actually work in the future. We can't control everything though because it takes up more time than it's worth so it's best to just focus on what works now.

The strategy I outlined in the chapter "Campaign Strategies" is reasonably straightforward and keeps things manageable by using one of each campaign type for each book. Over time you might decide to add more campaigns for ultra-targeted ads or possibly testing ad copy differences. If you are struggling to make your ads work or are quite new to this then it's best to keep things simple and easier to follow.

The Auto and category targeting campaigns are what I will generally use for discoveries. These campaign types are very broad and can find ASINs and keywords that we might not have thought of. The auto ads are particularly good for finding new keyword possibilities - the only problem with these campaigns is we have almost no control over them. Because of this, it's generally a good idea to make auto campaigns contain your lowest bids.

Over time, working with our search term reports we concentrate on auto and category campaign data to come up with a list of

ASINs and keywords that are working, or not working. We then add these to our product targeted campaign and manual keyword campaigns. All I'm giving you here is ideas. There's no right or wrong way of doing things. The only thing that's right is "are we making a profit". How we get there might work different for other advertisers, it might even be different between books and genres of our own. There is no single formula that's guaranteed and this is why you have to keep looking at the data, the time-lines and graphs to figure out what works. Whether you like it or not, you have to bring out your inner geek. What I describe here is one idea of many possible ways to do things but it follows a fairly logical rule: take information from campaigns that you don't have much control over - and put it into campaigns that you do have control over. The two campaign types we have the most control over are manual keyword and product targeting.

Let's say we have our four campaign types. We've researched and chosen keywords, categories and products that we think should work, setup the campaigns and let them run for a while to collect data. Maybe after a few weeks we look at the product, category and manual keyword campaigns to see if there is anything we should pause or perhaps lower or raise bids. We can view this directly from the advertising dashboard by clicking on each campaign and selecting the "targeting" tab, it's probably the quickest and easiest way. Next we take a look at the search term reports. We'll start by looking for ASINs that are getting clicks but no sales.

We can add these ASINs to the negative targeting list for our category ads. There is no point in negative targeting ASINs in manual keyword campaigns, it will only have any effect if somebody actually types the ASIN into the search bar, which will happen very rarely. Auto campaigns don't allow for negative targeting (at the time of writing), another reason why we keep the bids lower in auto campaigns.

Next we find ASINs that are working or look like they might have some potential with some bid adjustments. Remember this is all about efficiency. If an ASIN is working or looks as though it has potential then we want to negative target it in our category campaign. We do this because we can only make bid changes for entire categories so we prevent it from showing up there and then add it to our product targeted campaign instead, where it can be uniquely targeted and experiment with different bid amounts. If this ASIN is also showing up in our auto campaign then we can bid slightly higher than our auto campaign's default bid so that we can see how it performs. There's no guarantee that it will work better in the product campaign, even with a higher bid, but at least we have the option to try it and see.

Next we will look for search term keywords. These can require a bit more thought. Examples I give are for non-fiction but the principles remain the same for fiction.

Our (hypothetical) book is about playing piano for beginners. Let's look at some example keywords we might find are being used in our auto campaign. Our default bid is set at 0.22c.

"How to play piano" - 30 clicks / 2 sales
"Learn to play piano" - 18 clicks / no sales
"Beginners guide to piano" - 28 clicks / 3 sales
"Piano scales" - 42 clicks / no sales
"Piano scales for beginners" - 28 clicks 2 sales
"Piano scales poster" - 2 clicks / no sales

This might be the kind of data you will find in the search reports. There will also be quite a lot of keywords with very few clicks that may or may not have sales. These we need to ignore until we get more info over time, unless something stands out as very obvious, like possibly the last one in the list above. We'll get to that in a little while.

The first keyword "how to play piano" seems like a good keyword that's very relevant to our book. We would want to try bidding a bit higher to see if it improves sales. If you don't already have this keyword in your manual keyword campaign then we would now add it there and set the bid slightly higher than the auto campaign is bidding, we could try 25c or a bit more. Also, we'll make sure it's added as an exact match because what we see in the customer search terms of the search report is the exact keyword used.

The second keyword "Learn to play piano" doesn't look very promising. It does however sound like a good keyword so with only 18 clicks I would just leave it running longer before making a decision.

The third keyword "Beginners guide to piano" looks good and also looks like it could be quite profitable. I would put this into the manual keyword campaign (exact match) and maybe try bidding around 30c.

The next three keywords are where we need to think a bit more carefully.

"Piano scales" doesn't seem to be working, however, "piano scales for beginners" is working. What we could do here is to add "piano scales for beginners" as an exact match keyword and then add "piano scales" as an exact match negative keyword. Be careful not to add this as a negative phrase match because this would then kill the keyword that we do want to bid on, i.e., "piano scales" is a phrase within "piano scales for beginners".

The last keyword "piano scales poster," we could, if we wanted, add this as a negative exact match. An alternative might be to just prevent the word "poster" because it's unlikely people searching for a poster would want to buy a book instead. If, however, we just add the word "poster" as a negative phrase match then it will prevent any keywords that include the word

"Poster" from triggering our ads. Of course, this assumes that the above is correct and people searching for poster won't buy a book. As I've already said, we never really know for sure so unless it's getting a lot of clicks with no sales then it might be best to let it run for a while before we make that decision.

In Summary

Auto ads are great for discovering books and keywords. Some work, some don't. We have very little control over auto campaigns so will possibly end up paying for a lot of clicks that get few, or no sales. Because of this we keep the default bid fairly low and use the reports to find what is and isn't working. This will change of course if and when Amazon give us the option to add negative keywords to auto campaigns.

Category ads can get a lot of impressions and clicks. We have some control but only at a category level. We can however add ASINs as negative products. This means we can, along with auto campaigns, use category targeting to find ASINs that work or don't. Those that don't work can be added as negative products. Those that do work can also be added to negative products, while also adding them to a product targeting campaign where we have full control of the bid for each unique ASIN. Unfortunately at present this is a slow laborious job because we cannot bulk add these ASINs, they have to be added one at a time through KPD advertising. Hopefully they will see sense and change this in the near future, quite possible as it is an option on Advantage accounts.

Product targeted campaigns allow us to bid on unique ASINs. This not only allows us to experiment and monitor how they react to different bid amounts but also tells us the impressions, CPC, CTR etc., for each unique ASIN. This gives us more valuable data and a better insight into what other books are relevant to ours.

Manual keyword campaigns are similar to product targeting, the main difference being the use of keywords rather than product pages. We have a lot of control over the keywords, the only thing lacking is the ability to find out what product pages the keywords might have led to and we can't add ASINs as negative keywords (we can but it's pointless).

The reason we take good keywords and ASINs from auto and category campaigns is for better control. Let's say we are bidding 0.20c in our auto campaign and we discover a good keyword in the reports. If we put this keyword as an exact match into a manual keyword campaign, we can bid higher to see if we get more clicks and more sales. Sometimes there is a sweet spot - 20c might get some clicks and sales; 25c might work better, 35c work better still. 50c might continue to get more clicks but the AcoS may start to rise. The control we have in manual campaigns allows us to find this out. The same is true for category vs product targeting. By adding an ASIN to the negative targeting in the category campaign and adding it to the product targeted, we can experiment with bid amount per ASIN as opposed to raising the bid for the entire category.

This is all about experimenting. It can take many months to refine campaigns. Sometimes things work, sometimes not. We try something, we monitor it and decide what to try next. There will be times that things simply don't work as expected. For example, we might take an ASIN from a category campaign, use it in a product targeted campaign and even with a higher bid, it might not work at all. Sometimes the opposite will be true, we can move a keyword or ASIN into a different campaign and it goes way better than expected. There is no guaranteed formula or method that can be relied upon. People that have ad campaigns that work great - don't have it happen overnight. They watch everything, experiment and monitor the results. This is how it's done. What you do today might not work tomorrow. What works great now, might decline or stop working a few weeks later. Some things work great for a while and then stop suddenly. Some things work well and keep on working. Nothing here is set and forget. If you want to run profitable campaigns then you need to be watching them and making adjustments regularly if need be. The closest we can get to "set and forget" are auto campaigns so if all of this seems like too much for you, then perhaps auto campaigns are what you should use and then hope for the best, sometimes they actually work quite well so you might get lucky.

What if Nothing Works?

If you cannot get your book to sell no matter what you try, then something is wrong. You need to figure out what the problem is and fix it. You will need to think like a business and do what businesses do; invest and build a customer base, or in our case, readers. This might mean spending more than you earn while you build your reader base.

This is not a time to be a defeatist. It is, however, a time to be realistic. The first thing you must remind yourself is it's definitely possible to sell books. You do not need to be an established author with a large following and email list. Those that are will obviously have an advantage and sell much more than you. Don't allow yourself to think the other extreme means you are pushed out of the market and cannot possibly compete in their space. The only advantage they have is when you are competing in the same space, established authors are going to sell more than you most of the time. It may be that you need to spend more on advertising than they do: not because you will necessarily pay more for clicks but you might need more clicks to get the sale. If your book is good then this will get better over time as your ranking improves you'll get more visibility and the more you sell, the more chance of getting good reviews.

Like any other small business you will need to build your brand and customers, the most common way to do this is with advertising. Expecting a profit right from the start is great if it happens, but if it doesn't, it don't mean things are going wrong. Things are only wrong when you can't sell anything at all, or very rarely, or if you get a lot of bad reviews and possibly refunds. Every occurrence has a reason. Amazon advertising is probably the best way to find answers you can't get anywhere else, things like impressions and clicks vs sales which can tell us a lot about our book and how potential buyers are responding to it. If all else fails with your advertising, just think of it as payment for highly valuable information. When things aren't working, we use our advertising data to find out what's going wrong. Obviously you will need to have been running ads for at least a few weeks first, preferably a couple of months or perhaps spent a minimum one hundred dollars before you can collect any meaningful data.

Low impressions

We'll start with this one because if you aren't getting impressions then you have no other data to work with. If you have no impressions at all then something is probably wrong. You will often hear other advertisers talking about campaigns that "don't switch on". I've never had this happen myself but don't doubt that it does happen to others. I think there's probably an underlying reason if a campaign doesn't seem to activate at all, I doubt it's random, but who knows? I can't categorically state that it doesn't, I'm just a bit sceptical. Either way, if this does happen then simply run a few more campaigns with different keywords, categories and bid amounts.

Low impressions are more likely to occur than zero impressions, but either could happen for any of three reasons.

1: Bidding on keywords with low search volume
2: Bidding too low
3: Poor relevancy

Number one is simple, use different keywords. There's no reliable way to find search volume on Amazon, we can only use our own judgement. Try typing your keywords into the Amazon search bar and if it doesn't pop up as a suggestion then it's very likely to be one that gets low search volume. No amount of bidding can make it get more impressions, especially if you are using exact match.

Number two is fairly obvious and can affect all campaign types. It's easy enough to find out: just increase your bid, leave it a few days and see if the impressions start to increase. If that still doesn't work then try using the suggested bid for a few days.

Number three is a little more difficult. Relevancy affects all ad types and is harder to know if it's causing a problem. If you are using category targeted ads then as long as you are targeting relevant categories, you should be getting quite a lot of impressions if the bid is high enough. All other ad types might struggle more to get impressions if relevancy is off.

The problem with relevancy is it's not always you personally that is doing something wrong, it might be that Amazon itself has interpreted your book wrong and this is likely to be more of a problem with fiction than non-fiction. I've discussed relevancy quite a lot throughout this book so if you've been paying attention, you should know what to look out for, if not, go back and read the chapters on Relevancy and also the chapter "Running and Optimising your Ads".

Checking your book's detail page can give you some clues about what Amazon may think your book is about. Look at the categories your book is listed in and also look at the sponsored ads on your book's page. There will always be outliers shown but overall the books shown in sponsored products, also-boughts, also-viewed etc., should be generally in the same genre as your book. If not, you might have a relevancy problem. Check this on both your Kindle page and your paperback.

Impressions but few clicks

If you are getting a lot of impressions but few clicks then it will be likely caused by poor relevancy, a poor book cover or title, poor ad copy or too low bids. Let's start with the latter, low bids. The thing to remember here is an impression is not a view. If your ad shows up at the bottom of a page then you'll get an impression. A lot of shoppers, especially on search results pages do not always scroll down to the bottom of a page, therefore you get an impression but no actual view. This isn't necessarily a problem, people that do actually scroll further down a page might be more likely to buy because what they are seeing at the top is possibly not what they are looking for. As long as you are getting enough clicks then you shouldn't worry about it. If however you are getting so few clicks that the ad is essentially not performing then it's probably more likely to be caused by something else.

There's no typical click to impression ratio you should expect but a common consensus is that 1 click per thousand impressions is OK. This will show up in your dashboard and reports as the CTR (click through ratio). It's measured in percentage so 1 click per 1000 impressions will be 0.1% CTR. Just to give you an idea, my campaigns for the last 14 days currently show CTRs ranging from 0.07% for category ads and 8% for product targeted ads. My average CTR is around 0.5%. If you are starting out and are getting CTRs around 0.05% then you are probably doing something right, you just need to tweak them over time to get them working better.

Ad copy can affect click through rate. As long as it's on topic with the book then it shouldn't affect clicks drastically. Unfortunately we can't change ad copy once a campaign has been set. If you think your ad copy might be a problem then the best way to test it is to run another campaign without any ad copy.

The book cover and / or title can affect click through rate quite drastically. No matter how much you like your cover, it might just be wrong for the genre. People have certain expectations and often glance quite quickly through book covers and titles on search results and product pages. Making your book stand out among the crowd isn't always a good thing, although it can be, it still needs to grab the right attention. If a cursory glance makes the reader think it doesn't "fit" then it might have lost all chance of getting a second look. Same problem can happen with the book title. Don't try to be too different or too clever with covers and titles. If most of the best sellers in your chosen category all look very similar, it's probably for good reason. A poor cover isn't necessarily a bad cover, it can just be a wrong cover for the genre so don't get emotionally attached to it. Try another one, see what happens.

Apart from poor cover design, relevancy is often the biggest cause of too few clicks, the main problem being that your ads are simply showing in the wrong places ... or the right places but giving the wrong message. If it's showing in the wrong places then it could be that your keywords aren't well chosen or Amazon has the wrong idea about your book and what it's about. The keywords you choose should tightly match what your book is about, your search terms might be too broad or too far away from what the reader is actually looking for. Try typing your main keywords into Amazon and look at the books that show up in the search results, make sure they are very similar books. The Amazon algorithms already have figured out what types of books sell when certain search terms are used. Make sure your book fits in with the general results that show up. If it doesn't then your keywords might not be the best choice. The same goes for what product pages your ad appears on. You should be showing up on book pages that tightly match your book. If not, then you are either targeting non-relevant books or Amazon has your book figured out wrong. This may correct itself once you start getting sales, otherwise look for possible reasons why not, check the categories you are listed in and make sure the other books in those categories match yours.

Clicks but few sales

No sales or too few sales can happen for the same reasons as above but you get a little bit more info to work with and something to refine. You can't fix this problem quickly but you can usually improve things over time by refining your campaigns along with the data you collect from your reports. This is not necessarily something to worry about too much. Many advertisers start out their campaigns with high spends, to some extent it's to be expected. Achieving a low ACoS doesn't usually happen straight away. Some of my better performing campaigns have been refined over time, many months. If however you try to no avail and cannot get things to improve then it's likely to be your book description is not working very well, which you can fix by trying something different, or that dreaded word again ... relevancy. The thing about being relevant is it needs to work at every level.

Let's say that your book is a psychic romance suspense, then that's what it needs to appear to be at every step in the process from keywords to cover to category. If Amazon's algorithms categorise and assume your book is a psychic detective mystery, it will place your ads in those categories and show up more to people that usually buy that particular genre. If your book cover isn't making this obvious then it will get clicked on, the reader will then realise through the description that it's a romance book which is probably not what they are looking for.

Once your reports have collected enough data, it's wise to check out some of the ASINs and keywords that your ads are getting clicked from and make sure they are as relevant as possible. If relevancy seems good then it's almost certainly your book description that needs to be improved or changed.

Clicks too expensive

If you are in a competitive category then this is something you, to some extent, just have to accept. You may be able to get the overall cost down, again over time, by checking your reports and lowering bids or pausing ads for keywords and ASINs that are not converting very well. If the ads are working but just costing too much then first accept they are actually working. Think of this as an investment in your future readership. Obviously if the book is a one-off and you aren't writing very often then you might need to wait until you're ready. Many authors in competitive categories rely on read through for books in a series. The idea is simply to spend more advertising the first book in a series and make the money back from readers that go on to buy the rest of the series. Obviously for this to happen the books have to be good enough in the first place. If people aren't reading through then you are either selling to the wrong crowd or you will need to face reality, your books aren't quite cutting it. Learn from it and keep writing, work to make each book better.

Certain keywords and categories will always be expensive and you can't always get the cost down very easily, if at all. What you can do instead is try to improve your conversion rate. To some extent this will happen naturally. As your book sells more, Amazon will show it more in emails and in organic search which will effectively lead to free sales. If this happens then remind yourself that it has probably only happened because of the sales you have been making from those expensive clicks. When you factor this in, your clicks are effectively working cheaper. The same goes for reviews, if you get good reviews then you will likely make more sales. It's not easy to measure this with any accuracy but if your overall income is improving while your overall ad costs are about the same, then realise you are now getting a better conversion than you were before you were paying for expensive clicks. Think of it as pay now, earn later.

Experiment with different book descriptions and you might get the conversion even better. Do this with caution though, if a book is selling reasonably well, albeit with expensive clicks, changing the description will possibly force the algorithms to reevaluate your book. This may cause a dip to occur which you may or may not recover from. Unfortunately we are at the mercy of computer algorithms and can't predict how this might change things. You might have a new and tested description that outperforms your old one, but the algorithms could screw it up by now showing the ads in different places because they have changed the relevancy. If the book is selling OK but you really want to change the description anyway then it's probably best to make only subtle changes at any one time.

Final Thoughts

Everybody has their own way of doing things. There is no right or wrong method, only methods that work or don't. My method works for me, I make on average about 100% net profit over my ad spend and I don't rely on read through. It doesn't mean my methods will work for you but you should try them anyway. This will give you something to work with and refine. Read as much as you can, listen to everybody else and if other ideas make sense to you then try them. In the process you will learn a lot and settle on something that works for you.

There is no silver bullet. If you cannot sell your books then there is a problem. Every problem has a reason and a solution, you just need to find it. Always start with the simplest of analysis and work out from there. Advertising has become a necessary evil but don't think of it that way: think of it as paying for valuable information about how people are reacting to your book.

If you are getting impressions but very few clicks then there are only three possible reasons: either your book cover / title is not working, your ad copy is not working or you are showing up to the wrong audience or in the wrong places. No matter what you do to try to fix it, always remind yourself of the basis of the problem. It can only be one of those three things so they need to be addressed before you can move on. The first thing you could try is to run another ad with no ad copy (we know that books still get clicked on with no ad copy, if they didn't then also-boughts wouldn't be so popular). Now you only have two problems to deal with. Next, find where your ad is showing up and check out all the other books that surround yours. Are you absolutely sure you are showing up in the right places? If so, does your book cover stand out as different from the norm in that genre? Is it showing up right at the bottom of the page where people might not be looking? If you think something is wrong, change it. If you think everything looks just right then look harder because it isn't right. If it was, you'd be getting clicks ... assuming you are at least writing books in a genre that enough people are actually reading. If you aren't then there's your answer. This is how you need to be thinking every step of the way.

Same goes for clicks but no sales. If they click but don't buy then the problem is straightforward. Why would you click on something and not buy? You either decide it's not what you were looking for or you have been put off for some reason or you've not had your interest piqued. It's really that simple. Fixing it can be harder but you have to start by understanding the problem and breaking it down. Be critical. Is it possible that the cover gives a different impression than what's expected? Maybe your cover is telling one story and your description is telling another. Maybe people are reading your description and realising it's not what they thought it would be judging by the cover. Maybe they're reading it and feeling none-the-wiser or completely uninspired. Maybe you have some bad reviews and it's putting them off. If you do have any bad reviews, take notice of what they are telling you. Learn from it.

Every author and advertiser has their own methods. There is no single method that is "the only way". Read everything you can and try everything you can think of until you find what works for you. The only thing that's always right are the fundamentals. They never change so always use them as your guide to figuring out where your problem is.

The Fundamentals

1: People are not finding your book (no impressions)
Reason: Poor relevance, confused algorithms. Amazon can't figure out what your book is about or who to show it to.

2: People are seeing your book but not clicking.
Reason: Poor relevance, poor cover, poor ad copy, wrong audience or a genre / subject with very low readership.

3: People are looking (clicking) but not buying.
Reason: Bad reviews, poor relevance, poor description, wrong audience.

Nearly every problem you have will boil down to one or more of these fundamentals so come back and ask yourself these same questions repeatedly. If all else fails, keep writing and producing more books, maybe try a different genre. Don't give up and always ask others for critical advice. Listen to them and learn from it. Above all, just enjoy writing, you'll almost certainly get there in the end.